GUIDING THE CHILD

ON THE PRINCIPLES OF INDIVIDUAL PSYCHOLOGY

By Alfred Adler
and Associates

Translated from the German
By Benjamin Ginzburg, Ph.D.

Martino Publishing
Mansfield Centre, CT
2011

Martino Publishing
P.O. Box 373,
Mansfield Centre, CT 06250 USA

www.martinopublishing.com

ISBN 978-1-61427-148-2

Cover design by T. Matarazzo

Printed in the United States of America On 100% Acid-Free Paper

GUIDING THE CHILD

ON THE PRINCIPLES OF INDIVIDUAL PSYCHOLOGY

By Alfred Adler

and Associates

Translated from the German

By Benjamin Ginzburg, Ph.D.

LONDON

GEORGE ALLEN & UNWIN LTD.

MUSEUM STREET

First published in Great Britain, 1930

Printed in U. S. A.

CONTENTS

CONTENTS

PREFATORY NOTE

Under the leadership and inspiration of Dr. Alfred Adler, a group of physicians and educators have in the last few years organized twenty-eight child guidance clinics in Vienna, Berlin and Munich. Conducted according to the tenets of Individual Psychology, these clinics have revealed many new and stimulating problems that are as applicable to conditions in America and England as in the experimental countries. The procedure and results of the actual day-by-day work is given in this volume.

GUIDING THE CHILD is not a symposium. It is designed as an organized and connected account of the problems, accomplishments and failures encountered in the daily work, reported from actual experience by the experts in charge. Dr. Adler has edited the volume and assigned each subject to the specialist in that field, to the end that there may be no omission and no repetition. The result is a closely knit account of inestimable value to the welfare worker, the physician, and the forward-looking parent. The book does not sacrifice fact to popular appeal, but at the same time, it has been carefully prepared to meet the needs of the individual parent as well as the progressive group worker.

THE VIENNA CHILD GUIDANCE CLINICS

By

REGINE SEIDLER *and* DR. LADISLAUS ZILAH

THE first child guidance clinic along the lines of Individual Psychology was organized in Vienna by Dr. Alfred Adler. The example of Dr. Adler was followed by Dr. Leonard Seif, the chairman of the Munich Section of the International Association for Individual Psychology, who in 1922 established a similar center in Munich. Since then the number of such clinics has been rapidly growing, not only in Vienna and Munich, but also in other cities.

The establishment of the Vienna clinics owes its origin to a general need of social service as well as to a pedagogical problem. The enormous mental and material devastations brought about by the world war made it necessary for the state, for the communities, and for a large number of social and charitable organizations to turn their attention to the prevention of delinquency among children and youths. This task was approached with great understanding and devotion, especially in the case of the Vienna community and of certain other cities both in Austria and in Germany. If the work was not crowned with full success, it is partly because of the organizational defects of human society, partly because the methods employed for the discovery of the mental sources of delinquency and for the removal of the factors which cause delinquency, were not always the proper ones. It was Individual Psychology which threw proper light upon the sources of backwardness, delinquency, criminality; which traced the direct line connecting delinquency and backwardness with neurosis, and which thus discovered preventive methods in its pedagogy and therapy of encouragement. Individual Psychology naturally felt qualified to deal with these larger circles of children which are not reached by the customary agencies for social welfare, circles whose members as a rule do not deem it necessary to consult a specialist whenever they are confronted with backwardness.

THE VIENNA CHILD GUIDANCE CLINICS

The establishment of educational centers for Individual Psychology sprang from the conviction that the further fate of children suffering from backwardness, character defects, and delinquency, is above all determined by the enlightenment and education of their educators through the methods of Individual Psychology. The work of the child guidance clinic begins wherever the knowledge of the "professional" educators—of parents, teachers, and to a certain extent of physicians—is not sufficient to remove the educational difficulties of the child so as to encourage the child to remain on the useful side of life or to return to it.

That these clinics answer urgent needs, can best be seen from the interest which the Vienna teachers' and parents' associations take in them, constantly trying to increase their numbers. The fact that the importance of the pedagogical need—which was one of the factors in the establishment of our Vienna clinics—was recognized by a large number of the Vienna teachers as early as 1920, is proof of their understanding of educational problems, their professional idealism, their social sympathy and devotion. As a matter of fact, the stimulus for the establishment of the first Vienna clinics for child guidance came simultaneously from the Vienna teachers and from Dr. Alfred Adler. The necessity for establishing such clinics followed, for Individual Psychology, from its fundamental theoretical conception of the determining influence of education on character, as well as from its realization that given certain conditions educational failures must inevitably result. Many Vienna teachers who often had to work with backward pupils, applied for guidance and help in their difficult task to Dr. Adler, with whose work they had been familiar through books, lectures, and conferences. A new problem had emerged in Vienna on account of the recent introduction of compulsory primary school attendance, as well as on account of the great change in the attitude of the teachers towards the pupils brought about by the new type of cooperative manual school (*Arbeitsschule*), which took the place of the old disciplinary school. The Vienna teachers were confronted more and more with the problem of what to do with those pupils who do not advance in the schools which they are obliged to attend, and in which they form a disturbing element. The teachers turned for a solution of this problem to Individual Psychology. And in this way there were established in Vienna, clinics which were at first accessible only to teachers and to children introduced by them. The purpose of these clinics was to help the children and at the same time to enable the teachers to master the technique of Individual Psychology. Along with these clinics, which were designed primarily for training teachers and educators in the methods of Individual Psychology, there developed general guidance clinics which were voluntarily frequented, not only by teachers, but above all by parents and relatives with or without children, and also by children and youths alone. Individual Psychology in this way gained access, on a large scale, to the inner nature of the two factors which are of decisive importance in the education of most children: the school and the family.

Guidance is given free of charge in all Vienna clinics. The consultations take place in the early evening hours on certain days of the week. Each clinic is in charge of a physician trained in the methods of Individual Psychology, and of a medico-pedagogical adviser. The medical and pedagogical personnel is appointed by the committee of the Vienna section of the International Association for Individual Psychology.

Our experience with these clinics yielded such favorable results that we soon found it necessary to increase their number. Their increase was especially large in 1927. The constantly growing number of applicants for advice necessitated a corresponding extension and reorganization of the Vienna clinics. At present there are in Vienna twenty-eight child guidance clinics which are recognized and managed by the Vienna section of the International Association for Individual Psychology.

A detailed description of the technical side of these clinics will be found in the separate contributions to this series of articles. We should like especially to refer to those articles which deal with questions of the technique of child guidance; of the relationship existing between the clinics, the physician, and medicine; and of the relationship between schools and parents. Another interesting feature of these articles is to be found in the rehearsal of numerous cases derived from our practice.

The clinics directed by Dr. Adler are essentially teachers' guidance clinics. These clinics are chiefly attended by representatives of the teaching staffs of the primary schools in the various districts, as well as by the physicians, teachers, social workers and students, who are ready to learn and co-operate voluntarily. At the beginning of the school year a circular is sent by a representative of the Teachers' Guidance Clinics to the separate teaching staffs, calling their attention to the work of the teachers' guidance clinics and asking them to report cases of backward pupils. Each school in every school district is requested by the inspector of the respective district to send a representative for consultation to the teachers' guidance clinics. The teachers then report about their experiences to the teaching staffs of the various schools. In case a teacher wants to bring a pupil to the child guidance clinic, he first has to secure the consent of the child's parents. Whenever possible, the teacher appears before the advisers with the child and its parents. At first the teacher reports briefly, in the absence of the child and its parents, to the adviser and the students about the bodily and mental development of his pupil as well as about his or her home environment. After a detailed discussion of the case, the child and its parents or guardians are called in. When the consultant is through with the child, he again discusses the case in detail, suggesting practical means for the removal of the child's difficulties, and pointing out the connection of the given case with the fundamental tenets of Individual Psychology. The conversation with the teacher and parents, and the subsequent discussion of the case are especially important because the future treatment of the child is left by the teachers' guidance clinic to its parents and teacher. The latter have to exercise the proper educational influence in accordance with the ideas suggested to them. The success of the guidance work—the transformation of the child and the disappearance of his difficulties—is largely determined by their proper understanding and grasp of the case. The teacher especially tries henceforth to influence the child and his parents, with whom he remains in constant contact. The home environment of most big-city children makes the teacher the center of gravity in education.

It is true that in a number of cases the home environment of the child forms an obstacle that is almost impossible to overcome. It is therefore easy to understand the fact that most guidance workers would like to see the establishment of *educational homes accessible to every one and conducted on the basis of Individual Psychology.* Such homes would have to be in immediate contact with the child guidance clinics. They would thus offer an opportunity for individual treatment to those children in whose case a temporary removal from the customary environment would insure the success of the guidance work. After the successful termination of the treatment the child would return to its parents. Meanwhile the parents would be prepared for the proper continuation of their new task by evening lectures and consultations. During the child's stay at the educational home he would also be taught those subjects which prevented his advance at school. The far-reaching significance of such a training in social usefulness is especially shown in the article on "School and Educational Guidance." Of course, these homes must not bear the odium of institutions for correction; they have rather to assume, in the eyes of the public, the aspect of recreation homes.[1]

In accordance with the special aims of the teachers' guidance clinics, the child as a rule appears for guidance only once. This is, however, not the case with child guidance clinics. Here the guidance worker tries to gain the confidence of the child and the parents by means of mild enlightenment. In this way he is able to induce them to come spontaneously to the guidance clinic until the child learns to overcome his difficulties. The child is, for instance, stimulated to perform certain definite tasks, and later he comes gladly by himself in order to report about the work he has done. Often the treatment is carried out with the help of assistants trained in the methods of Individual Psychology. The child is in this way dealt with privately, and when necessary he is tutored in his school subjects. The assistants, on the other hand, have

1 The educational homes existing in Vienna, Berlin, and Munich, are private institutions and hence not accessible to the general public. There is, however, in Vienna, an afternoon center based on the principles of Individual Psychology.

thus a chance to get an insight into the home environment of the child and to influence him to a certain extent.

The above-mentioned distinction between two types of educational guidance clinics is a purely external one, inasmuch as no applicant for guidance is ever sent back by either type of clinic. The applicant is at liberty to come as often as he likes. This loose distinction has today only a historical meaning, going back to the manner in which the clinics were organized. It perhaps also serves the purpose of facilitating the way to the guidance clinic for those who are interested in its work, especially to enable separate categories of professional educators to come together in certain guidance clinics as students. It is obvious that the kind of guidance which deals with the child alone can accomplish its end only very seldom, only under specially favorable circumstances. In every case, and in all guidance clinics, we have to aim to secure, as far as possible, the co-operation of all contributing educational factors.

The adviser in these guidance clinics has to satisfy certain rather high requirements. He is confronted with the difficult task of grasping the life-plan of his fellow beings almost instantaneously (a thing which is rendered much easier by the mastery of Individual Psychology), and of exhibiting the error underlying this life-plan in such a convincing manner that it becomes evident both to the child and to his educators. To be able to accomplish this, one has to turn to the technique of Individual Psychology, of which Dr. Alfred Adler says that it is not only a science but an art. We cannot enter here upon a detailed account of the principles of Individual Psychology. We can only point out that our educational guidance, just like any education based on Individual Psychology, begins whenever it is a question of recovering one retarded function for the child or two retarded functions for the mother. When the consultant converses with the child, he must first awaken in the latter the feeling that there is one absolutely reliable human being on whom he can count under all circumstances; second, he must lead the child from his experience of one fellow being to the community, and assure his organic incorporation into human society. Through contact with the child, the guidance worker's task of unearthing the source of the fundamental error in the life-plan of the child is rendered easier. Since the backwardness and the character defects of the child are to be explained by errors in his education, the question of confidence also plays a great part in regard to the parents and educators of the child. The very attempt to seek guidance already involves a certain measure of confidence. The success of the guidance, however, depends upon the degree of insight possessed by the educators. In the guidance clinic the child sees that he is surrounded with people who treat him as an equal. Here he is not only not scolded for his mistakes, but he is, on the contrary, shown how he has erred, and he is told that there can be no obstacle in the way of his return to the useful side of life. The conviction thus forces itself on the child (just as it does upon the parents and educators): *"I am here in the presence of a person who means well by me."*

The adviser will show that the moment of the appearance of the first difficulty in the education of the child coincides with outer and inner psychological difficulties that confronted the child at that time. The failures of the child will be proved to be a result of a defective preparation for certain definite situations. The child then becomes freed before his own eyes, as well as before those of his educators, of the oppressive sense of guilt, since he is encouraged to do useful work. The discovery of the source of the errors enables the child's relatives and educators to gain a better understanding of him, to assume a more correct attitude towards him and to arrive at proper educational methods. The consultant will have to pay special attention to the encouragement of the applicants for guidance, to the encouragement of the child and his educators (parents). The hope of a better insight entails a peace of mind which was previously disturbed by the consciousness of an error or of a failure caused by an erroneous goal. The child and the educator must not leave the guidance clinic without the inner conviction: *I can enter upon a new road.*

The first step towards a communal experience is already brought about by the establishment of frankly human relations between the guidance worker and the child. There is also another factor at work in our guidance clinics which is especially apt to make the child feel his relationship with the community. The work in our child guidance clinics proceeds in most cases with the doors wide open. The public character of these clinics has often been attacked. Our experience has shown, however, that the appearance of the child before a large gathering—that is to say, the public character of the guidance—has a stimulating effect upon him. The publicity of the procedure suggests to the child that his trouble is not a private affair, since strangers are also interested in it. His social-mindedness is more awakened through this. The child realizes that he is surrounded with people who take a great interest in his fate and difficulties, without looking down upon him and without forcing their help upon him. If he were to witness an emphasis upon "guilt," he would naturally have an aversion for the publicity of the guidance. He is, however, treated with confidence and as an equal; he finds that his inability to meet his tasks is regarded here as something temporary, as due to an error and as by no means a guilt. Under such a treatment the sense of self-respect is not hurt, and we therefore have no reason to give up the publicity of our educational guidance, which we regard as a means for stimulating the social feeling of the child. The public character of the guidance clinics is furthermore a means for training professional educators in the art of bringing up healthy and courageous human beings; it is a device for avoiding the most frequent, the most dangerous, and the crudest educational errors. Everyone who has had experience with educational guidance confirms the fact that the publicity of the treatment often entails immediate social, material, or mental help for those who come for guidance. And this certainly is a factor which is most valuable from an educational point of view as an example of social sympathy and readiness to help. It goes without saying that we do not insist rigidly upon the publicity of the treatment, since compulsory measures are incompatible with the fundamental principles of Individual Psychology. The treatment thus occurs privately whenever the person to be guided desires it so, or feels offended by the publicity, or whenever the discussion of delicate problems is involved, or finally whenever the special conditions of the case require the exclusion of publicity.

In giving a condensed sketch of the therapeutic and educational activity of our educational guidance clinics we do not ignore the danger involved in a schematic representation. Such a schematic representation offers, however, a certain practical advantage; it enables one to get an insight into the inner workings of educational guidance. It is with regard to this practical advantage that we shall comprehend the activity of the educational guides for Individual Psychology under the following four headings:

1. Securing the confidence of those who come for guidance.
2. Discovery of the sources of educational errors.
3. Encouragement.
4. Stimulating the social sentiments.

Each of the four phases is indispensable, and success can be achieved only by working with all of them. A treatment, for instance, which fails to discover errors in the life-plan, can secure an apparent success only. Even if the acute symptoms of backwardness have disappeared for a time, others are inevitably bound to appear.

Besides these four aspects our educational work exhibits another feature which has, according to our conception, a determining influence upon the future of the child: the education of the educators.

The significant growth and success of our educational guidance clinics entitle us to great hopes. It is naturally not in our power to fill out the gaps resulting from the defective organization of human society or from a lack of insight into the significance which the school and the home have for the education and future of the child. The therapy and pedagogy of encouragement offered by individual psychologists will remain ineffective as long as the encouragement given in our guidance clinics is counterbalanced in school and at home by repudiating, degrading, discouraging, and condemning the child. The recent progress in the domain of social welfare as well as the change in the pedagogical attitude of the teachers entitles us to believe that we are drawing near the end of the time when the child and professional educators have had to depend merely upon the voluntary, sporadic, charitable enlightenment offered by the guidance clinics. At a time when the social service of the state, countries, and communities tends more and more to embrace the entire population from babies to old people, the demand for extending this work to mental welfare will also become obvious. More and more will the necessity be felt for applying Individual Psychology to the training of parents, vocational educators, teachers, officials, judges; in short, of all those who have to deal with children and education. The future of the educational guidance clinics for Individual Psychology points in this direction.

THE PHYSICIAN AND EDUCATIONAL GUIDANCE

By

DR. OLGA KNOPF *and* DR. ERWIN WEXBERG

IT is an old experience that physicians, especially pediatrists, are constantly confronted with educational problems in their daily practice. Also it is a familiar fact that the large majority of pediatrists are not sufficiently prepared to meet these problems. Education is not included in the curriculum of our medical schools. Thus, even the most experienced pediatrists are, in regard to pedagogy, more or less qualified autodidacts. They derive their knowledge of education either from experience with their own children, or from an old practice in which they have learned from mothers and nurses what they are supposed to impart to other mothers and nurses. This obvious gap in medical training can of course be excused by the fact that before the development of Individual Psychology there scarcely existed a system of education that was either practicable or teachable.

This excuse can hardly be regarded as valid today. The knowledge gained by Individual Psychology clearly shows the soundness of the demand, not only for co-operation, but also for a personal union between the physician and the educator. It will not do to allow the pediatrist, who as a rule is regarded by the family as an absolute authority on all questions concerning the child, to combine medical knowledge with ignorance in educational matters. The theory and practice of educational guidance upon the basis of Individual Psychology must be given a proper place in pediatric training.

This relation, however, is a reciprocal one. If the physician cannot dispense with educational knowledge, educational guidance on the lines of Individual Psychology must absolutely depend upon the co-operation of the physician. There is hardly a case which does not involve, besides pedagogical aspects, specific medical problems.

These problems are first of all of a diagnostic nature. A child makes himself conspicuous through great motor restlessness. The teacher tries to check the bad habit with the customary pedagogical devices. Finally, the parents are referred to the guidance clinic. It is for the physician to ascertain the source of the trouble. It is possible that we have to do here with one of the usual bad habits in which spoiled children occasionally indulge in order to get attention from the people surrounding them. It may also be that it is a question here of chorea minor (St. Vitus dance), an organic nervous disease which manifests itself in involuntary movements of the whole body. It would not be easy to decide here, since choreatic motor disturbances tend to pass, within fluctuating limits, into bad habits. Nor will the school physician be able to make an unmistakable diagnosis after a single examination. A similar problem is offered by digestive disturbances, which play such a large part in the case of very young children. Constipation, vomiting, lack of appetite, are frequent symptoms of gastric troubles. But all these manifestations are equally the results of a bad education. There is a special complication here owing to the fact that these disturbances, even if they spring from mental sources, can lead secondarily to pathological changes in the functions of the organs. In this way, we become involved in a vicious circle which it is not always easy to burst.

Of no less importance is the psychiatric diagnostic in educational guidance. Children are again and again referred to the guidance clinics in order to ascertain whether they are feeble-minded and whether they had not better be sent to a school for backward children. We know to-day that not very much is to be expected from intelligence tests. If the child solves tests appropriate to his age, we can quite well establish that there is nothing wrong with his intelligence. In case, however, he fails to solve them we cannot ascertain the real cause of the failure. It can lie in feeble-mindedness, but it can also be looked for in a mentally conditioned factor, such as discouragement, called forth by the environment of the child and by the resulting bad training. The source of the trouble can be determined here only by a physician trained in Individual Psychology and inclined to pay careful attention to the whole personality of the child and to the environment in which he has grown up. It generally lies in the direction of psychogenic thought-inhibition with normal intelligence, as can be seen from the following cases:

Case I. A nine-year old boy, a pupil of the fourth grade of public school. He had been sent at the beginning of the school year to a school for backward children, and since this experience made him very unhappy, he was put back into the regular school on probation. But since reading and writing apparently give him unsurpassable difficulties, he is supposed to go back at the end of the term. His reading has improved somewhat since the beginning of the term. But nothing can make him read even a single letter when a stranger, be it another child, is present in the classroom. He is the youngest of three brothers, the two other brothers being considerably older than he. He is a decidedly pampered child. The outstanding trait of his character is cowardice. He avoids fights, and when attacked by his comrades he runs to his mother to complain. At home his parents have no difficulties with him. The examination reveals good bodily development but a latent left-handedness which had not been noticed before. Upon inquiry the mother admits that previously the child had always to be exhorted to use his right hand, and that even now he uses his left hand in polishing the floor.

Since conversation with the child offers no ground for inferring that we have here a case of mental defectiveness, we are justified in assuming that the difficulties in reading and writing are partial manifestations of a general lack of courage. From an etiological point of view the decisive facts in this case are: left-handedness, the position at home of the youngest, late-born child, and a pampered bringing-up. The guidance clinic had accordingly to declare itself against sending the child to a school for backward children.

Case II. A seven-year-old girl, pupil in the first grade of public school. The child is unsociable in the school, beats her comrades and spits at them. She has not learned to read or write. Of late, to be sure, she has begun to show a slight sign of progress. Despite her unsociability the child is loved by her comrades. Here, too, the question of sending her to a school for backward children was raised. The mother of the child died of tuberculosis, and for a year and a half now a stepmother has been in the house. The child is also tubercular. A medical diagnosis had already pointed to a cerebral lesion as the cause of her unsocial behavior. The girl is the oldest of three children, and she does not harmonize with the others, since comparisons are constantly made which are not in her favor. Our guidance clinic has come to the conclusion that the possibility of organic deficiency cannot absolutely be excluded here. It has, however, found, that on the whole, we have before us a child who has failed to adjust herself socially, owing to certain environmental influences (loss of the mother, wrong pedagogical attitude on the part of the stepmother and father). Her recent improvement makes it unnecessary for her to be sent to the school for backward children. After four weeks the teacher was able to report that the child displayed considerable progress in her achievements so that she could remain in her regular school.

The practical significance of such successes of our guidance work must not be underestimated. There can be no doubt that to send normal children to schools for backward children—a rather frequent occurrence—means to interfere with their development in a very serious manner. And this alone is apt to give educational pessimism an artificial confirmation by making the child which has been regarded as feeble-minded secondarily feeble-minded.

Organ inferiority plays a more determined part in the life of children than in that of adults. This shows itself either in the feeling of discouragement resulting from handicaps created by such defects as left-handedness (case I), or in the gradual lowering of the sense of self-respect caused by general diseases like tuberculosis (case II), status thymicolympaticus, etc. An organic disease often serves as a signal for the appearance of mental troubles. The manifestations of the disease are here put to the service of the neurosis, and in this way they are unconsciously aggravated and made part of the psychological style of life.

Case III. A twelve-year-old girl, a child born out of wedlock. At the age of a year and a half she fell out of her bed and allegedly hurt her spinal marrow. At present she suffers from rheumatism in her joints, walks slowly, and is not allowed by her mother to go out in bad weather. The child grew up with strangers, and has been living with her mother only for the last few years. She has a much younger sister, born of her mother's present marriage. The child is a bad eater, does not like to help in the house, and feels she is discriminated against in favor of her younger sister. At school she disturbs the classroom work, and does not get along well with her comrades. But strangely enough, she participates in gymnastic exercises and feels hurt when she is put out of the ranks—a fact which contradicts her alleged rheumatism. She is quite well-versed linguistically, reads much, and writes poetry. She wishes to become an actress. It has been noticed that her rheumatic pains become especially intense whenever she wants to obtain something from her mother, and that, as a rule, her tactics are successful. Her mother accordingly is advised not to take her daughter seriously. She is also instructed how to bring up her child so as to make her socially adjustable. After four weeks the child is again brought to the guidance clinic. We learn now that during all this time there was no mention of rheumatism.

The psychological situation, and especially the further course of this case, do not entitle us to assume any important organic basis for the alleged pain. But on the other hand we must not ignore the fact that real organic diseases and congenital defects play a large part in the mental development of the child as well as in the genesis of educational difficulties. To deal adequately with such cases involves for the physician both diagnostic and therapeutic problems. The treatment of such diseases as rickets and its after-effects, of glandular and bone tuberculosis, and of after-effects of infantile paralysis is of primary importance in this respect. For all diseases which check the normal growth and the normal motor dispositions of the child, or which impair seriously the external appearance of the growth through crippling or maiming, give rise to organ inferiorities which the child tries to meet in a manner made familiar by Individual Psychology. The serious discouragement falling to the lot of a child with spinal curvature will sometimes defy pedagogical influences exercised with the best of intentions. If the defect, however, is removed or essentially mitigated through timely orthopedic treatment, then the goal of the educator will also be won. We have also to refer here to infirmities which are perhaps unimportant from a medical point of view but which may become psychologically disastrous, since they disfigure the external appearance of the child. The correction, for example, of a distorting abnormality of the teeth must therefore be regarded by no means as luxury. Those who have seen how greatly children and young people in general suffer from the consciousness of ugliness, how such a feeling can give rise to serious inhibitions of the social sense, to distrust, even misanthropy, will certainly not underestimate the importance of the collaboration of medicine and pedagogy in this domain.

Diagnosis and therapy, however, are not the only tasks which confront the physician in his educational guidance work. He has to perform a third function which is perhaps more important than these two. We have in mind *enlightenment.* It is a question of correcting a multitude of dangerous notions about medicine deeply rooted in the minds of the lay public—notions having a baneful influence upon home education. The popularization of medicine, which of late has assumed enormous dimensions, involves, besides the numerous useful services rendered by it, many dangers which must not be overlooked. They can be partly explained by the fact that the medical knowledge of the lay public usually remains, for obvious reasons, considerably behind the progress of scientific medicine. In this way it happens that medical views which had been valid twenty or thirty years ago, but which have since been discarded, seem right now to get a firm foot-hold among the lay public. This is, for instance, true of the concept of "nerve weakness" (neurasthenia) which was coined by Beard in the second half of the nineteenth century. At that time this concept stood for an "irritable weakness" of the central nervous system—brain and spinal cord—in short, to an over-straining of these organs as a result of sexual or other excesses. In case of the so-called constitutional neurasthenia the basis was supposed to be supplied by an inherited disposition. Despite the fact that the force of inertia controls the development of concepts in the domain of scientific medicine, we can certainly maintain today that this old concept of "neurasthenia," with its partial manifestations of "cerebral" and "spinal" irritability, is no longer taken seriously by scientific medicine. We are nowadays at least aware of the enormous influence exercised by psychic factors upon all those phenomena which are still subsumed today under the collective concept of neurasthenia. We realize more and more that psychic causes occupy the first place also in the genesis of these symptoms. But despite the scientific modification undergone by this untenable doctrine, the discarded concept of "nervousness" as a bodily disease still haunts the minds of laymen and educators. It may be granted that this erroneous conception is at least useful educationally insofar as backward children considered as "nervous" are no longer beaten as much as they used to be at a time when their "nervousness" was regarded as mischief to be extirpated by the rod. It is nevertheless evident today that the assumption of neurasthenia in the case of a child is equivalent to a partial or complete resignation on the part of the educator. The view that all possible failures on the part of children are to be reduced to nervousness is very enticing to educators. It offers them an opportunity for mitigating their responsibility and for excusing themselves for results which are in reality nothing but the failures of their educational methods. This soothing self-exculpation is henceforth inevitably transferred to the child who is ready to cloak every failure at home and in school, every act of intemperance, every neglect of duty, with the mantle of nervousness. We cannot discuss here the baneful part played by this convenient tactic in the life of adults, making them idealize defects of character which could have been removed through education or self-education had it not been for the pretext of nervousness.

In this connection we should also like to mention the mischief of certain lay theories of heredity. These, too, come from the second half of the nineteenth century, from a time when the materialistic conception of nature had reached its zenith. Although we owe to this conception numerous valuable scientific advances, it is also responsible here and there—especially in the domain of psychology—for many retrogressions. We cannot enter here upon a scientific discussion of problems of heredity. We can only refer to the ludicrous misunderstandings to which these questions give rise in the minds of laymen. A mother of two children thus asserts that she has inherited not only her great nervousness but also a strange form of a difficulty which she experiences while getting up in the morning. She is able to leave her bed at every hour of the day or night, at three, six, eight o'clock, but not at seven. And curiously enough her children have the same difficulty; they, too, cannot leave their bed at seven o'clock, an hour which is most proper for getting up in order not to be late at school. Certainly no better testimony for heredity can be desired. It does not, however, occur to the naïve mother that the children may be simply imitating her.

We are all familiar with weighty discussions about the hereditary source of the nose and eyes of a three-day-old baby. Does the former come from the father and the latter from the mother, or vice versa? Similarly the character of older children is carefully analyzed into parts, each trait being explained by a hereditary prototype among relatives. A child thus has his talkativeness from a cousin of the mother, his laziness from a great aunt, his insolence from a paternal grandfather, his lack of aptitude for calculating from a maternal uncle. It cannot be denied that such fallacies of the theory of heredity, which purposely ignores environmental influences, are not quite dead yet, even in official science. From a psychological point of view, this persistence can be easily accounted for. As a rule, it enables parents who are familiar with the theories of heredity to lay the precedent for the failures of their child at the doors of their ancestors, and on the other hand, to ascribe his positive qualities to the excellent education they gave him. Educators, owing to their great fear of responsibility, avail themselves of the theory of heredity whenever a pretext for pedagogical failures is desirable. This fear of responsibility, too, is transmitted—to be sure, not in a hereditary manner—to the children. In this way we can understand the following answer given by a boy of fifteen to his father who had reproached him for his bad school marks: "I cannot help it. With such an abnormal shape of the skull as I have, one cannot learn well, and this shape of the skull I have inherited from you!" Ten years later he told this in the course of a psychotherapic treatment which was necessitated precisely by his neurotic fear of responsibility.

This shows how important enlightenment is in educational guidance. It is evident that it can be accomplished only with the help of the physician's authority. It is the physician who will above all succeed in removing deeply rooted prejudices. No one will be more successful than he in instructing the parents that the alleged inheritance of a nervous family tradition rests upon an illusion, that heredity plays here a nonessential part, and that it lies in their power to break with the tradition for the sake of their children.

Finally we have to mention another domain where medical enlightenment forms an indispensable element of educational guidance. We have in mind sexual education. As is well known, this is the field of the most mediæval of prejudices. Suffice it to mention one fact. The enormously exaggerated dangers of onanism still play a baneful part in home education. The great horror experienced by parents upon their discovering signs suggesting that their child indulges in onanism springs from their own sexual fears. It has been pointed out again and again that the superstitious fear of the possible consequences, which thus communicates itself to the child, is infinitely more dangerous than onanism itself. Yet parents persist in clinging to their beliefs, unless they are convinced by a specialist to the contrary. And quite often even the authority of the specialist does not carry much weight, for such a disgusting, horrible, immoral practice, it is felt, must involve harmful consequences. The scientific views and pedagogical methods of parents thus mirror their own philosophy. If defects of character are in this way transmitted from generation to generation, we certainly have no right to shift the responsibility to heredity.

We believe that we have shown in this brief account that educational guidance on the lines of Individual Psychology cannot dispense with the collaboration of physicians trained in pedagogy. Let us be fully aware of the responsibility connected with the work of guidance. It is a question of applying the most efficient method for the prevention of delinquency, criminality, and neurosis. As it happens, the experience gained from practice enables the doctor to foresee the results that are likely to follow from the apparently harmless seeds of a childhood dismayed through lack of guidance. It is he who is so familiar with the horrorful mass of misery, wretchedness, and guilt which comes to light in the collapse of adults and which weighs upon future generations with the force of destiny. It is therefore the physician who above all has to lend a helping and preventing hand to the work of child guidance.

WHEN TO REFER CHILDREN TO GUIDANCE CLINICS

By

MARTHA HOLUB *and* DR. ARTHUR ZANKER

THE following types of children should be sent to child guidance clinics:

A. In the *nursing age* all those cases which are usually characterized as neuropathic or "bad" children, for both prophylactic measures against neurosis and direct educational guidance can be applied in the first year of a child's life. To the first group belong all the so-called nervous and functional diseases of the nursing age with the various manifestations of over-stimulation of a sensori-motor and vaso-motor nature. Prophylactic guidance and enlightenment of mothers is required here, especially in the case of eating difficulties, the eating neurosis, the eating strike, nervous sleeplessness, dentitio difficilis, and respiratory spasms. Special attention is, however, to be paid to the second group of the "bad" sucklings who may already manifest results of a mistaken education. We have in mind, for instance, the well-known cry-babies. Putting aside the part which feeding and nursing may play in this respect, we have to ascribe the blame above all to pampering (constant rocking and carrying around). Of special significance in this connection is the great anxiety shown by parents, their fear lest their baby catch a cold; in short, the all-too-warm psychic home atmosphere of the baby. Prophylactic education is one of the most important tasks here. Finally we have to point out that for all somatic cases (such as birth-traumas, encephalitis, lues, hydrocephalus, debility) as well as for all other early noticeable abnormalities (myxodem, mongolism) it is advantageous to establish an early intimate contact between the mother and the child guidance clinic.

B. In the age of *infancy* all those cases are noteworthy which, apart from the neuropathic manifestations classed under *A.*, are characterized by disorders in behavior, for the first educational difficulties date precisely from this period. Special difficulties are now frequently encountered in connection with the attempt to train the child to empty his bowels and bladder at will, to eat, wash, and dress himself without the help of others, to relieve his parents or nurse at the proper time, and to adjust himself in general to society. Wrong education in this respect expresses itself most often in such pathological symptoms as enuresis, pavor nocturnus, disorders of all kinds which prevent the child from falling asleep, vomiting, onanism, playing with excreta, etc. Disorders in social adjustment resulting from a bad education assume such negative forms as stubbornness, defiance, fits of rage, aggressiveness, isolation. Both the above-mentioned pathological symptoms, as well as the so-called mischiefs, equally require the intervention of the child guidance clinic.

C. In the *school age* we find, apart from the disorders classed under *B.*, the manifestations of backwardness in learning, which is an expression of a general defective preparation on the part of the child. Defective preparation shows itself at this age not only in the form of failure but also in the most varied symptoms of backwardness. (Here belong the well-known types of peace-disturber and rebel, the buffoon, the liar, the thief, up to the highest degrees of dissociality and a-sociality, as well as the types of the timid-fearful, the phlegmatic-disinterested and the self-sufficient model child.) With this backwardness both of intelligence and character we have to regard the numerous nervous symptoms, of which the most frequent at this age are nervous vomiting, neurosis of the stomach, rectum, heart, generalized and localized tics, somnambulism, etc.

D. In the age of *puberty* and *pre-puberty* we are confronted specially with conflicts of a sexual nature, and with difficulties at home and in the choice of a vocation. It is through the help of the guidance clinics that the dangers of neurosis and dissociality can be prevented at this stage. Special attention is here required for the manifestations of dissociality and incipient delinquency, which assume the forms of vagrancy, frequently of gangs; addiction to alcohol and nicotin, suicidal attempts, and prostitution. As to the neurotic symptoms of this age, medico-educational guidance finds a fertile field in the various "hysterical" and "hystero-epileptic" diseases, the psychogenic neuralgias, the basedowoid psychic disorders, the akne juvenilis, the psychic disorders in menstruation, homo-sexuality, and sexual perversions.

Apart from our classification in accordance with age, definite groups of children can be put in a common category insofar as a contact with and periodic observation by a child guidance clinic is important for all of them. To this category belong all orphans and wards, found both in private and public homes, illegitimate and step-children, and children of divorced parents or of parents about to be divorced. To the class of children that are especially menaced by environmental dangers are to be referred all "only" children as well as all those that are enmeshed in particularly unfavorable family constellations. Another prime indication for the necessity of a contact with a guidance clinic is furnished also by the existence of any organ defects, as defects of sense organs (weakness in hearing or seeing), disorders in the organs of speech (stuttering, stammering, deaf-mutism), disorders of the alimentary canal (Herther's infantilism), and constitutional deviations and abnormalities in the secretions of the ductless glands (giantness and dwarfishness, adiposity, eunochoid). The latter indication deserves special mention on account of its intimate connection with important mental reactions and also because of the possibility of medico-pedagogical aids.

THE FAMILY AND EDUCATIONAL GUIDANCE

By

DR. ALICE FRIEDMANN

EDUCATIONAL problems have now become all the more acute and difficult to solve when children are compelled and are even spontaneously inclined to participate in life earlier and more vehemently. A pedagogical method which would protect youth and at the same time make it independent is not generally known. Owing to the pressure of economic conditions and the demands of modern times, which consume patience and leisure, it is also difficult to protect youth. Adults transmit the sense of pressure and the struggle becomes reflected in the children. The modern organization of education seldom results in a harmony between the educators and the educated, although they both suffer from the same evil.

Under the existing disharmony the obvious help is from the outside. Children look forward in any case to the outside world, unless they are too discouraged. It is difficult for the family to extricate itself, without outside help, from the ring of oppressiveness created for it and by it. But despite all this, a pedagogic guidance center, even if it can co-operate with the school, is confronted with the difficulty of intervening in a state of affairs which the family regards as personal and as concerning nobody but itself. Educational guidance clinics accordingly have to conduct their investigations and guidance *in a personal manner, but without personal motives.*

This aversion on the part of the family arises not so much from any serious considerations as from its mode of life. Families from which nervous children come often live in complete seclusion. It is because of this tendency to seclusion that they are reluctant to discuss matters of inner life, and consequently to apply to guidance clinics for help. Such families thus prefer to keep the backwardness of their child within their own four walls. There are various factors at play here: there is the fear of outside interference, there is the distrust in strangers, there is also a false sense of shame that such a thing as a backward child should occur at all in the family. Above all, what justifies this attitude in their own eyes is the fear that the world may learn of something—be it poverty, sickness, hereditary burdens, addiction to alcohol, mistreatments, or a mere trifle—which they regard as a hidden evil, as something capable of disgracing them. The complete discouragement which haunts the homes of very backward children expresses itself in one refrain: *it would not do any good anyway.*

To overcome this mood, to decide to apply for advice to a proper place already means much. The success of the guidance work, however, can be greatly hindered by the attitude of the parents. Their nervous disposition often expresses itself in the fact that they aim at something different from what they actually admit or what they clearly realize. Under the mask of parental love and of pedagogical scruples they try in the guidance clinic to enhance their own prestige and to discredit others, even their own child.

We often hear it said, and with good reason, that it is foolish to blame oneself for sins of omission. Nevertheless, such an attitude on the part of parents is hardly conducive to the welfare of the child as it involves too much distrust in the future of the child and in the efficacy of educational methods. It is closely related to the method of self-defense which forms the heart of parental testimonies, and in which an attempt is made to show that everything is done for the child. In accordance with the ego-centric tendency of neurotics, parents aim to show that they are not so bad as one might infer from the condition of the child. One step more and one hears the mother begin to talk about her own virtues, burdens, diseases, etc. For the success of the guidance work it is important to offer parents an opportunity for expressing themselves about their own troubles, marriage, etc. In this way we are able to get an insight into the parts played by the actors in this domestic drama, as well as into the connection existing between the backwardness of the child and the neurosis of the grown-up members of the family. The nervousness of the child is brought forward as a proof of one's own disease or of that of the marriage partner. The child is thus played off against one of the partners, who is made to realize that he has a sick child with whom nothing can be done. In their search for supporters of this opinion they make the guidance clinic a court of appeal. Before this forum the parents of badly educated children appear with unsurpassable principles. Much better informed than the school, they try to show that the latter can do nothing for their child, insisting upon this despite their previous statement that the clinic was their last hope.

This brings us to the very difficult type of parent whose methods are directed against the child. Through the guidance clinic, the child is to be intimidated, frightened; he is to be shown that he is incorrigible. These parents reject all responsibility, which is shifted to someone else. The disposition of the child is to blame for everything. Self-exculpation often has close affinities with ego-centric ideas.

All the above-mentioned cases offer a fertile soil for neurotically distorted and false statements. The intention of saying nothing or of not saying everything is often obvious from the very beginning. Many false testimonies are cases of self-defense, others betray an attitude of superiority towards the adviser. False statements due to a tendency for self-protection are frequent. Such statements are not always directed against the child. Colored reports are resorted to by parents also as a way of escaping or of helping the child escape the burdensome guidance business.

Bad intentions sometimes change during the guidance session. This happens especially as a result of personal ingenuity which unravels the situation of the child, or in consequence of the remarks of the adviser which suddenly give a new turn to the initial point of view. The parents often realize during the guidance session that they ought to imitate its tone. In this way they suddenly begin to point out, in their narrative, the good traits of their child, which they do not notice otherwise. They also feel that a helping attitude meets here with the greatest appreciation. The testimonies are important psychologically. The fact is that the truth content is not the only thing that matters here. There exist other indications and means of proof. Testimonies are often given in order to veil or misrepresent real conditions. They are also often given with a view to enabling the adviser to see through them. This happens with statements made at the guidance clinic for special reasons; for instance, in cases where the parents want to suggest that the child is not being utilized for a certain purpose, or where they want to get rid of the child, or where they wish to obtain material help.

It follows from the nature of our guidance work that the adviser cannot be a truth-fanatic, that his aim is rather to get hold of every opportunity to help the child get ahead. Of course, the more of the truth he gets the better. He must also possess a sense for the inarticulate play which sometimes takes place between him and the parents. It is against the spirit of our guidance work to shame them. On the other hand, in certain cases protection is won for the child through the fact that the parents feel that their intentions are clearly penetrated. As an illustration we can mention the case where a mother tries to induce her daughter to become a prostitute. An open disentanglement of such a situation would give rise to a most violent scene. This may be avoided and better results may be obtained through mere inarticulate suggestions, and above all through the fact that those who co-operate in the guidance work keep the child in mind. The efficacy of this inarticulate and sympathetic method will specially justify itself wherever measures of control can be applied. In other cases the effect of the exposition of the true state of affairs is also incontestable.

With these remarks we do not intend to deny or minimize those cases where the attitude of the parents contributes largely or materially to the success of the guidance work. The admission that errors have been committed, recollections of the parents' own childhood, experiences with the elder children, the realization that this method is better than that, and above all the despair—"I cannot put up with the child's condition any longer"—all this brings out the truth and offers the strongest help to the factual testimony.

The simultaneous presence of the child and the mother constitutes a source of enlightenment concerning the domestic atmosphere and the home life of the family. The child that moves in the guidance clinic in the mist of maternal love —plays with the mother, who gets the word out before him and speaks in his stead. The child that is in open conflict with his mother is militantly challenged by her "to tell everything." The child who has lost every hope of having his way at home immediately attaches himself to the adviser, disregarding the nagging mother who openly reproaches him for his utterances and behavior. The tyrannized child looks towards the mother whenever he is asked a question, the mother answers for him, giving a perfect exhibition of the home life, and threatens to push the guidance work into the background. The manner in which the mother cries and the child laughs, or the way in which the feigned indifference is gradually given up throws a great deal of light on the character of their relations. This shows itself best through the appearance of the other children of the family.

Besides these clear insights our guidance work also yields impressions of a less distinct nature which some people may be inclined to characterize as intuitive. They probably result by way of inference from numerous small indications. It is in this way that we obtain a picture of the home atmosphere. During our conversation with the mother and our examination of the child's school accomplishments, we suddenly realize how indolent and stagnant everything must be in their home, where they are all chained to a narrow circle from which there is no way out. Sometimes the picture of an utterly disorderly life dawns upon us, a life which can give no security to the child.

Our guidance work can be said to have accomplished its aim only when it has enabled the participants to gain a better understanding educationally. The immediate effect of the guidance work upon the family may at first be of the nature of a disturbance. Everything depends on the force of the impression and also on the ability of the family to assimilate and adapt itself to the new ideas. This assimilation and adaptation will not occur in case the vanity of the family has been hurt during the consultation and in case the sense of co-operation has been destroyed, as for instance, when each parent tries to win the child in his own way for himself. In other words, in case the backwardness of the child is so interwoven with the nervousness of the family that its members are no longer interested in removing it. If the wife shows that she is overburdened by the backwardness of the child and the husband utilizes this as a proof of her inability to cope with the situation, it will be hard to persuade them of the possibility of improvement, or of the necessity of being more critical towards their own attitude and of changing themselves accordingly. The confusion of relations, the distrust, and discouragement are here in the way.

On the other hand, apparent obedience is also not in harmony with the spirit of guidance work. People who are accustomed to impose their will upon others try to utilize the methods of Individual Psychology to satisfy their claims to superiority. Our method has a much better chance of success in case it is to all appearances flatly rejected. Of course vanity will give this success a different name, claiming that other factors have been at work in the improvement. Even in the most difficult cases it is improbable that our guidance work should remain without effects. If only one piece of advice is followed in a difficult case, a misfortune is likely to be averted. If the sense of responsibility has been awakened to such an extent that the child is no longer beaten, that he is not always discouraged, that he is sometimes spoken to in a kind way, we cannot say that we have here a curative pedagogy. Nevertheless, this can give so much joy to the parents and child that a host of successes may follow in its wake, especially if the school lends a furthering hand.

If we win only one person in the family, if we succeed in inspiring him with hope and confidence, the short course of our treatment at the guidance clinic may then really lead to an education. The reduction of worries to natural limits, the relief offered by the possibility for giving utterance to one's troubles, the new opportunities and the general human point of view which divests the misfortune of its particularity, really create a spirit favorable to education.

The reconciliation with the child is the first condition which the family must satisfy if it is to achieve co-operation. Far from expecting a regeneration of the family, we are nevertheless entitled to look forward to a revision of many a habit. Not to beat and degrade, not to pamper, not to keep in a state of dependence, to admit to every form of activity, to overlook mistakes and acts of defiance, to offer every chance for reconciliation, co-operation, for making amends, to foster sociability and all the forms of training suggested by our clinics—all these rules, even if they are obeyed rather sketchily, are of great pedagogical importance. If they are adhered to strictly and in detail, they bring the family a real understanding of the proper development of their children. If a change in the environment can be effected, these rules have a chance to be carried out with a lesser resistance and with a greater success.

THE SCHOOL AND EDUCATIONAL GUIDANCE

By

OSKAR SPIEL *and* FERDINAND BIRNBAUM

THE concept of "manual school" has undergone various changes of meaning. Understood originally in the sense of participation in manual labor, the concept of work soon assumed an absolute meaning. For Kerschensteiner [1] this concept denoted a school "which, through its methods and the form of its whole structure, releases the immanent values contained in its subjects of instruction." Hugo Gaudig [2] vindicated the ideal of a freely creative spiritual work whose aim is the unfolding of personality. The personalistic pedagogy of Gaudig and his adherents lacked, however, the constitutive character of social reference. It was left for Paul Na-

1 G. Kerschensteiner, Begriff der Arbeitsschule. Leipzig, Teubner.

2 Hugo Gaudig, Die Schüle im Dienste der werdenden Persönlichkeit.

torp [1] to fill this gap. The ideal of instruction and education was formulated by this thinker as fitness not only for life in society but also for one's own participation in the further development of society. In this way a higher and more ideal connecting link was furnished for all manual school reforms: *education for social life.*

The Berlin congress of 1928 showed clearly that it is this idea of social education that is foremost in the minds of the teachers. The problems with which they have to grapple—the transformation of the methods of instruction into the spirit of the work-and-problem school, the releasing of the spontaneous powers of the child so as to enable him to determine his own problems, methods, and the necessary means of solution, the stimulation in the child of a critical attitude towards himself and towards the work accomplished by him—all pointed in this direction. The teacher who is seriously concerned with reform problems could not fail to realize that his task as an instructor could fundamentally be solved only by laying greater stress on the educational side of his activity. He had also to

1 Paul Natorp, Sozialpädagogik. Berlin, Springer.

recognize that what we need here is not an interference "from above" but a realization that the difficult problem of the social life of a school class could, just as well as instructional problems, be worked out in the course of time by the children themselves. The success, however, of the co-operative activities of a school class has been questioned all too often. There can be found in all school classes children who—to use current terminology—have no "aptitude" for arithmetic, and who constantly interfere with the other pupils owing to their own defective accomplishments. We are all familiar with the peace-disturber who derives pleasure from disturbing and hindering the work of the class, with the buffoon who is ready to play a silly trick at the decisive moment and in this way to paralyze the energy of the other members of the class, with the bully, and similar types. It is these intractable children that render the solution of the problem of social education so uncommonly difficult. One is almost inclined to say that the problem of educating for social life is identical with that of insubordination. To change these intractable children, that is, to incorporate them into society, to make them useful members of the community, is the wish and aim of all teachers.

Small wonder that Alfred Adler found an attentive and enthusiastic audience for his ideas among the Vienna teachers. This fact soon led to the establishment of educational guidance clinics for teachers' co-operative groups. The meetings, which usually take place twice a week, are called together by the chairman, announcements being sent to each school in the district. A member of the teachers' group brings an intractable pupil of his class to the meetings and reports about his history. This gives rise to a detailed theoretical discussion, in which an attempt is made to find a connection between the facts of this particular case and the general truths of Individual Psychology, such as organ inferiority, left-handedness, the role of the mother, the idea of playing safe, the formation of the secret life-plan, etc. Thereupon suggestions follow as to how to proceed practically in the given case. Finally the meeting is led to the "guidance proper," which again offers an occasion for fruitful discussions.

It is hardly possible to exaggerate the significance of these teachers' co-operative groups. Again and again the teacher has a chance to recognize the enormous part played by courage in the dynamics of psychic life, the paramount importance of encouraging the child, and the utterly discouraging effect of the attitude of an authoritatively inclined educator. This realization will not only have a favorable influence upon the teacher's own behavior—the atmosphere in his class will become warmer—but it will also communicate itself through discussions and conferences to numerous teachers who are not in direct contact with the co-operative groups.

One who knows the part played in the life of a child by the experience of a defeat in his tasks will apply all his efforts to make such defeats impossible. In case defeats are unavoidable the teacher will encourage the child and help him to come back to himself.

A teacher trained in the methods of Individual Psychology and familiar with guidance work will have a proper understanding of what it means to have aptitude. He will realize that so-called stupidity is a means for getting out of work; he will consequently look with different eyes upon the "stupid" pupils of his class—often identical with the socially hostile, and he will thus avoid many an error in his treatment of them.

We are thus entitled to make the following statement: The significance of the teachers' guidance clinics lies primarily in the fact that the practically trained teacher has learned to avoid many mistakes in the education of children. This already means very much, as everyone who is familiar with conditions knows. Individual Psychology in this sense is a technique for avoiding mistakes. Individual Psychology is accordingly prophylaxis.

Backward children are often evaluated from an ethical point of view. We have only to think of the famous mark for conduct, popularly known as a mark for morals. According to a widespread opinion, this mark forms not only a value judgment but also an excellent educational device, since it has the effect of a deterrent, and besides, induces the parent to intervene "educationally." Individual Psychology is all too familiar with this "education." Many parents and teachers, it is true, try to change such outside methods, but current methods of sermon and rod fail in most cases, since they do not touch the heart of the problem. In his search for help, the educator turns to the various systems of psychology, where he finds detailed descriptions, valuable facts, interesting "typeologies," clever definitions, acutely formulated rules. He misses only one thing—an answer to the question: "What shall I do in the given particular case?" Koffka [1] certainly is right when he says that it is not the task of psychology to make statements about the child X or the child Y, but about what is common to all children. Practical workers must have the courage to say: If this is the case, then the study of character is more important for us than that of psychology, although we should not neglect the latter. This was emphasized by no less an authority than W. Wundt,[2] who was of the opinion, "that the study of character is more advantageous to the teacher

[1] K. Koffka, Die Grundlagen der psychischen Entwicklung. Ostercireck, Zickfeldt. English translation, The Growth of Mind, New York, Harcourt, Brace.

[2] Walter Seidemann, Die modernen psych. Systeme und ihre Bedeutung für die Pädagogik. Leipzig, Jul. Klinkhardt, p. 61.

than that of systematic psychology." This explains why so many teachers have turned of late to "interpretative psychology." This psychology stands nearest to characterology, and seems to offer rich perspectives. But even here the old story repeats itself: things are here catalogued and classified into types, and again no answer is given to the most acute of all questions: "How is this particular situation to be changed?"

Individual Psychology also tries to understand appreciatively. The very purpose of the inquiry into the antecedents of the child is to enable us to assume the point of view of the child and to regard the world, as it were, through his glasses. But Individual Psychology at the same time gives an answer to our question, and the answer is: Reveal to the child his erroneous life-plan, which he has drawn in false perspective, encourage him, and lead him back through proper training to the useful side of life.

The Vienna teachers have learned from their experience with the guidance clinics that this answer of Individual Psychology is presented there not as a demand but as a practical exercise. In the guidance clinic the teacher sees *how the thing is done.* The gain of the teacher is thus a double one. In the first place he learns to really "understand" the children. He becomes acquainted with the various forms of flight to the useless side of life, with the senselessness of security arrangements; he realizes the significance of the fictitious goal of superiority; he gets an insight into the dynamics of psychic life; he learns to regard human character as an expression of a compromise between self-assertion and social-mindedness. But above all, he learns to understand the profound saying of Alfred Adler: *"Human character is for us never a basis for moral evaluation, but a social fact."* In this way, the teacher learns to assume quite a different attitude towards the problem of backwardness. When the teacher has learned to regard such children not as degenerates to be evaluated morally, but as merely misguided, then, and only then, can we say that the indispensable presupposition for pedagogical activity has been created. The success entailed by the guidance work constitutes a source of encouragement for the teacher himself, and inspires him with that optimism which springs not from illusions but from a deep insight into the workings of the inner life. It is this insight that gives that tranquillity, that self-possession, which so much facilitates the direction of a school class.

But the second gain which the teacher derives from his experience with the guidance clinics is of a higher order. He not only learns the art of inquiry, of interpretation, of meaningfully harmonizing the most contradictory traits, but above all he learns to discover the vitally dangerous errors of children, he learns to take apart their securities, he learns to inspire them with courage and to begin their proper training for life. So we see that this second significance of the teachers' guidance clinics is the fact that the deep understanding gained through them leads to living activity, that they truly mediate between the *theory* and *practice* of Individual Psychology. The "revolutionizing practice" cannot be learned from books or lectures. Let it be said frankly: He who learns Individual Psychology only from books and lectures will know it as a science, but not as an art. Individual Psychology is both a science and an art.

He who works practically knows how necessary it is often to change the home situation of the child, and how difficult it is to induce many parents to come to a guidance clinic where they may have to talk before a large forum about intimate matters of family life. On the other hand, an educational influence has often to be exercised upon the parents also, and even the most careful beginning gives them stage fright, with the result that they refuse to come a second time. Shall the children therefore be left without treatment? The Vienna teachers who are experienced in the art of Individual Psychology try hard to awaken among parents an interest in our guidance clinics. For information in regard to this point we may refer to the article on the significance which parents' associations have for guidance clinics.

Ferdinand Birnbaum distinguishes in his article "Technique of Education"[1] five formal phases in the treatment of backward children: 1. Establishing contact. 2. Disburdening. 3. Analysis of problem. 4. Setting up of a new task. 5. The solution. The fourth point seems to

[1] Sophie Lazarfeld, Technik der Erziehung. Leipzig, S. Hirzel Verlag, 1928.

offer the greatest difficulties. Here is an instance.

E. was a pupil of the first class of the public school. From the first day he was invariably late at school. He used to open the door quietly and steal in. He stood before us with colorless eyes, and in a whispering timid tone, the stereotyped answer came out of his mouth: "I got up too late."

His things were never in order. He seldom brought any exercises and even when he did have one, he did not venture to hand it in. He sat bored and indifferent, and his eyes were often directed towards his neighbor's note-book in search for help. He never took part in the conversations of the pupils. His accomplishments at school were defective, his writing and form were beneath criticism.

His mother was in despair. She had the hardest time to make him get up in the morning; he was totally devoid of any spirit of independence. But in addition to all this he was insolent, rude, had a "knows it better" attitude towards his mother, and was uncommonly aggressive towards his brother, four years his junior.

It is not very difficult to establish contact with such a child, to disburden him, to reveal to him the fundamental error in his life-plan, and to encourage him by proper words. But while he hears from his adviser that he, too, can do things, his own experience shows him that he cannot fulfill the requirements despite his efforts. Therein lies the difficulty. It is a question here of granting the child a period of grace and of initiating a systematic training in order to fill the existing gaps. If the teacher does not have the proper attitude blamable situations will always arise to discourage the child, and all the efforts of the adviser will lead to no favorable results. This is corroborated by many instances. The teacher alone can manage the situation so as to enable the child to achieve success.

The teacher has the three best compositions read aloud as samples. From other compositions he reads before the class fairly successful passages only. He does this in order to give E. an opportunity to read aloud a passably successful sentence. In this way the teacher is instrumental in making the child realize that he too can do things.

The question of systematic training becomes more and more acute in the degree that our institutions expand and progress. If we wish to achieve something more than short-lived changes, we must solidly anchor the child to his new mode of life. We must make him immune to feelings of inferiority which may arise from new dispositions to inferiority. Only if we keep this principle in mind will it be possible to avoid a serious danger closely connected with this training. We shall be able then to prevent the training based on Individual Psychology from degenerating into a sentimental effeminacy, from becoming a source of fears of possible infections by feelings of inferiority. We can hardly hope to realize this training in the case of children by means of guidance work alone. It is necessary here to enable the child to become more courageous as he proceeds from task to task, until he is in a position to retain his sense of self-respect even when he is confronted with problems which he cannot solve (the "courage to face imperfection," as H. Lazarsfeld calls it). Therein lies the crucial experiment, and only systematic training can show the way.

In systematic training we must always take into account the peculiar nature of the collective work of the class. It is not sufficient, for instance, to bring home to a child how to perform a certain case of division. We must train the child to adapt himself to the methods of procedure used by his class—and these methods are nowadays different in different classes, since they depend on the initiative of the class. But it is only the teacher, as the organizer of the collective work of the class, who can determine what a pupil needs in order to get along in a class having definite interests and definite methods of work. The teacher thus seems to us to be the most qualified person for the task of guidance work; it is he who is at the same time revealer, guide, trainer, director.

Many teachers, followers of Individual Psychology, have drawn the necessary consequences. We accordingly now have a third variety of guidance clinics, whose sphere of activity is, to be sure, limited to pupils of a class—namely, class guidance clinics. Three or four times a week during office hours the teachers put themselves at the disposal of parents. Otto Glockel, the president of the Vienna school council, has coined the expression "consultation hour." It is high time to translate this ideal demand into facts. We must not satisfy ourselves any longer with the fact that defects exist, but we must try to find out why they exist, and must finally endeavor to discover ways and means of removing them. The teachers are confronted with great problems. If schools are to become educational schools, and if the ideal of education for society cannot be attained through influencing collective life—however important such an influence may be—they must precisely concern themselves with the individual treatment of the more difficult cases, and this in the spirit of guidance work.

This, however, means an additional burden. It is not the place here to draw professional conclusions. The lively interest which the public takes in educational questions offers us a guarantee that more and more attention is being paid to educational maxims. The existence in Vienna of guidance clinics on the basis of Individual Psychology raises for the teachers entirely new problems which demand a solution. Suffice it to mention here only one instance. W. is a "hated" child. At school he represents the type of the bully. What attitude does the sense of justice of the children assume towards the fact that one of the rude acts of W. is brought up during his period of grace for discussion before the class? It is after all impossible to analyze before the children home situations which may explain the behavior of W. but which are also liable to throw a dubious light upon his parents. Certainly there are possibilities for adjusting the tension. At any rate an important problem is involved in the contrast: individual treatment—mass education. It seems to be easier for girls' classes to cope with such a problem than for boys' classes. The latter have rather a predilection for a form of organization in which mathematical justice prevails, and they seem to retain this attitude even after their educators have tried again and again to unmask this literal conception as unjust. The more members a social aggregate has, the more mechanistic will be its spirit, the more will it try to conform to literal justice. This means that limits will be set to educational influence by the number of pupils—limits that will be valid also for the educational expert. It is this point which explains so clearly why teachers demand "day homes," on the basis of Individual Psychology, for backward children.

The spell of an age-old tradition is beginning to break down. The Vienna child guidance clinics have thus become stimulants to a new development whose further course it is hard to foresee. The "educational science" of the past was able to offer to the practical educator nothing better than the obviously trivial advice of striking a right balance between severity and kindness. It is only psycho-analysis and, quite separately, Individual Psychology that have really been able to offer something decidedly new. Our guidance clinics in this way have become something more than guidance centers; they have become transformation centers and driving powers. Like all driving powers, they lead more and more to new forms of organization. The wide chasm between home education and education in educational institutions must be bridged by intermediary institutions.

THE INFLUENCE OF INDIVIDUAL PSYCHOLOGY UPON PARENTS' ASSOCIATIONS

BY DR. THEODOR ZERNER

WHEN the downfall of the old regime paved the way in Vienna for the long-demanded reform of the schools, it became apparent that it was necessary to win over the parents to the new cause. It was this idea that gave rise to the Vienna parents' associations. These are associations of the parents of a given school, having for their purpose the creation of a better understanding between the school and the home. Every month the parents come together with the teachers of the school to discuss matters concerning the school and the children. The teachers have spared no efforts to bring home to the parent, by means of lectures and practical talks, the new methods of instruction and education. In this way the teachers have been able to gain a contact with the parents of which they never even dreamt before. This work soon made both teachers and parents realize that the reform of the schools will be completely successful only when the home of the child will change fundamentally its attitude towards educational problems.

Apart from this, more and more people have come to realize that the old disciplinary methods of education with their rewards and punishments will no longer do. New ways are being sought in various directions. We cannot describe them here. We may only say that recent economic development has changed to a certain extent the old system of division of labor, and has shifted the educational basis accordingly. Besides the father, the mother also has often to work for a living outside the home. Families with one child are more and more frequent. In many families, the child knows an idle father and a mother who quite often has to regard the management of the house as an additional but unnecessary burden. A disciplinary education will under such circumstances naturally be felt as oppressive; over-indulgence and pampering, on the other hand, prepare difficulties for the child at school.

The general interest in all kinds of educational problems becomes every year more and more intense in Vienna. It was thus natural to expect that the parents' associations would soon concentrate their chief interest on the enlightenment of the parents in regard to educational problems and that they would in this way become a favorable soil for the practical dissemination of the educational methods among the wide masses of the population. Much work has been accomplished in this respect. Physicians and teachers trained in the methods of Individual Psychology give lectures before the parents' associations. Their activity gives the parents a feeling of relief. The district unions, that is to say, the combinations of the parents' associations of all the schools of each Vienna district into a single union, establish more and more guidance clinics which have a double purpose. They offer help to distressed parents and children, and give enlightenment to the audiences. These parents' meetings form a proper forum for the discussion of educational difficulties, problems connected with backward children, social education, as well as for the popularization of the methods of Individual Psychology and of the ideas of the guidance clinics. The district parents' association of the twentieth Vienna city district, for instance, has organized this year for the second time a parents' guidance school where for six or seven evenings an introduction is given to Individual Psychology. Of the twenty-seven schools and five kindergartens of the district the course is frequented on the average by three or four parents' councils, and this means an average attendance of ninety persons. In this way there is no school in this district in which at least some parents have not been initiated into the ideas of Individual Psychology. And these parents often induce us to give in their schools, for the benefit of all parents, lectures on educational problems from the point of view of Individual Psychology. This naturally results in a higher attendance at the guidance clinic maintained by the district parents' association. The work of organization and enlightenment carried on by our teachers assumed such dimensions last year that for weeks the guidance clinic was compelled, owing to the excessive attendance, to open an annex.

It is to the self-devotion and relentless activity of the teachers and guidance workers that we owe the fact that there is at present at least one guidance clinic in practically every Vienna district, where parents can get advice and help. Also the union of the Vienna parents' associations publishes a magazine "Home and School," in which pedagogical problems are treated from the point of view of Individual Psychology. In the articles written by teachers, cases mostly from the practice of the guidance clinics are utilized for pointing out errors committed and for suggesting methods of treatment. In this way all the work of the Vienna parents' associations becomes more and more permeated by the spirit of Alfred Adler's Individual Psychology, its practical applications being popularized among the wide masses of the Vienna population.

PROPHYLACTIC EDUCATIONAL GUIDANCE IN PARENTS' ASSOCIATIONS

By Olga Knopf, M.D.

It is well known that many parents refuse to bring their children to the guidance clinics, because they believe that the child, and hence they themselves, are being arraigned there, or because they think that no one can understand their child so well as they can understand it themselves, and that guidance is therefore useless. To remedy this situation, it is important to win the parents over to the idea of guidance work at a time when they have no immediate reason for applying for help, that is to say, at a time when they can regard educational difficulties and methods of removing them in an impartial, objective and disinterested manner. In the monthly meetings of the parents' associations the parents have a chance to discuss fundamental questions and difficulties in a free spirit. In this way light is thrown on many prejudices and confusions which would offer a greater resistance to removal later on, at a time when the parents will be confronted with an educational difficulty of their child.

It has become customary for those schools whose committees are in sympathy with the aims of Individual Psychology to invite the managers of the respective guidance clinics to give lectures at parents' meetings. The interest in these lectures is so great that in most cases continuations become necessary. In this way courses on pedagogy along the lines of Individual Psychology can be arranged for parents. The introductory lectures are followed by discussions. The parents put various questions which are discussed and answered. In this way the parents learn from practical examples which they themselves bring forward, how to deal with their children and how to utilize the advices given in the course of the discussion for nipping in the bud or for preventing small transgressions on the part of their children. It is a real joy to see how eagerly they come and how at the next meeting they report about results of their own accord. These introductory courses are in reality prophylactic guidance. If at a later date there should come up before the audience the case of a specially discouraged child, the parents would gladly bring this child to the proper guidance clinic in accordance with the advice given to them. In this way our guidance clinics are filled with material at the end of the course, whereas at the beginning newly established guidance clinics often have difficulties in inducing the parents to bring their children.

For this work of enlightenment we have to be grateful to the Vienna teachers and school directors, who spare no time and effort to win the sympathy and support of the parents for our cause. At the parents' evenings most of the teachers of the respective school are present. It is easy to obtain from a teacher additional information in regard to a child in case the report of the mother before the parents' association is insufficient or not clear. In this way co-operation between parents, teachers, and guidance workers has really been secured in many cases, to the advantage of the child. We have naturally to point out with regret that among the participants of these meetings there still are many parents who remain deaf to our ideas, because they cannot emancipate themselves from the principles of disciplinary education.

I should like now to make use of the minutes of one of the meetings of the parents' association in order to show how far the parents have advanced in understanding the mental life of their children and how they have learned to avoid conflicts with the children.

This meeting opened, like all others, with various inquiries. Several mothers came up, reporting about minor transgressions on the part of their children and asking for advice. As luck would have it, four women complained about the same "crime," and it was interesting to see how they themselves regarded the matter. All the four women reported that their children had a predilection for snow and waded in it. The coincidence is easy to explain by the abundance of snow that winter. Cases from daily life are an excellent means for showing the importance of enlightenment. The explanation of such cases is much more fruitful for parents,—consisting as they do for the most part of officials, employees, laborers,—than a whole series of the most beautiful theoretical lectures.

The first mother reported in an excited tone: "The child had the grippe, and no sooner did he get out of bed than he ran down and went straight into the snow. I told him ten times, before he went down, not to go into the snow; he promised me solemnly to obey, but as soon as he reached the street—I watched him from the window—he plunged into the heap of snow and came home wet up to the knees. And you, doctor, say that the child should not be spanked. How am I to manage the boy?"

The behavior of the mother showed clearly her militant attitude towards the child as well as towards myself. She called forth a feeling of resentment in all the people present, since she gave me no chance to speak, constantly interrupting me. Finally I succeeded in establishing the following fact. The eight-year-old child feels that he is being discriminated against in favor of his five-year-old sister, he acts disobediently as a protest against the supposed discrimination. He is the leader of his comrades and he tries in this way to satisfy his sense of superiority, since he is considerably suppressed at home. The behavior of the mother at the meeting suggested that she was a woman of quite domineering disposition. Probably the grippe is still for the boy a source of pleasant memories, because during his illness his mother showed him more tenderness than ordinarily. During his illness he must have been the most important person and he is not quite averse to having the same situation repeated again.

Immediately after the discussion of this case there appeared a second woman with the following report. Her boy who is nine years old had also been coming home for several days wet, after wading in the snow. The first day the mother said nothing and the next morning gave him another pair of shoes for school. A few days later he again came home all wet. The mother then said to him: "You have spoiled two pairs of shoes. If you wet your third pair, you will not be able to go to school, since you have no more dry shoes. Besides, you know that it is not easy for your father to spend so much money."

Thereupon the child took off his shoes and

stockings, took the stockings to the stove to dry, and since then he has been coming home with dry feet. The mother emphasizes the fact that her behavior was dictated by experiences in our lectures.

The third mother described the following scene. As she was going for a walk with her eight-year-old boy, the latter noticed a dog rolling in the snow. He then asked the mother whether the dog was not cold, and the mother answered that the dog's skin is his garment, and that he is therefore protected against the cold. The following day the boy came home from school covered with snow from head to foot. When the mother wanted to know what had happened, he answered in an embarrassed way that he had fallen down.

The mother said jokingly, "I guess you have not fallen down at all; you have simply imitated the dog."

The boy looked at the mother dumbfounded. In the first place, his mother was at this moment to him a sort of clairvoyant, and in the second place, instead of the greatly feared scolding, he was given a sensible criticism. The boy laughed, the mother also, and the situation was thus saved. The mother added: "But you will have to clean your shoes and your clothes yourself." Without saying a word the boy undressed himself and cleaned his clothes and shoes. From that day on the behavior of the boy on this point gave her no reasons for complaint. The mother concluded her report: "At first I found it difficult to follow your advice and to resort to a criticism dictated by the situation, but I see the success, and everything is all right now."

After this, there came a fourth case. This time it was presented by a father. He reported: "Nothing is of any avail, the boy wades in the snow. Punishments, words, exhortations, make no impression upon him. He does not even mind being excluded from our family outings on Sunday, and left alone at home." (We can quite well imagine that the child would rather stay at home alone than join an outing where he is constantly being "educated.") The child goes so far in his attempts to reform that he offers his father his purse before they start out for a walk. "You can keep it if I go into the snow again," he says to his father. No sooner does he say this than he is in the midst of a big heap of snow.

I try to explain to the father that the child at least makes efforts to show his good will. The father insists that only by means of beating can something be accomplished. I do my best to persuade him that beating is only the price which the child has to pay for his pleasure, for the expression of his self-assertion; that beating, far from being a means for correction, offers the child an additional stimulus to seek again his pleasure. Here the mother of the child came up and said: "You are perfectly right. When the boy goes out with me, he says to me: 'Mother, let me have my portion of blows now, then I can at least go into the snow.' "

The absurdity of the value of blows certainly needs no better proof than this. Further comments are unnecessary.

These lectures at the parents' meetings offer an excellent opportunity to combat effectively all kinds of educational prejudices and superstitions before large audiences. In the same evening, for instance, a mother of a ten-year-old girl came up with the following story: The girl sucks her thumb and in such an intensive way that "the thumb has become quite thin." All educational measures have proved futile. She, however, knows the source of the trouble. During her pregnancy she once saw a child who sucked his thumb. It is thus evident that this impression transmitted itself to the child!

The answer to the innateness and immutability of this trait was given to me by a father who told the following story about his two boys. One of the boys, who is twelve years old, had a habit of pulling his eyelashes whenever he listened to a thing with interest; the other, who is ten years old, constantly moved his hand under his nose so that his upper lip used to become all black during the day. Neither kindness nor severity seemed to change matters in the least. But under the influence of our lectures he finally decided to ignore these bad habits. He is now glad to report that the older boy has stopped pulling his eyelashes and the younger one has no longer any black marks under his nose.

The parents' meetings thus show the gratifying results of our daily pedagogical work. Prophylactic enlightenment given in proper time is able to prevent errors and difficulties in home education, which would otherwise require a bigger apparatus for their treatment, and which also would yield slower results.

Another little experience from the same evening. In connection with the faults of the abovementioned children I pointed out that the struggle between parents and children leaves unmistakable traces even in advanced age. By way of illustration I referred to the case of a man who is forty years old. This gentleman lives with his mother apparently in perfect harmony. Whenever a fresh tablecloth is laid on, the mother never fails to say: "Look out, we have a fresh tablecloth, be so kind as not to make any spots!" . . . There is immediately a spot on the tablecloth. The man assured me that this happens against his will, that he tries very hard to be careful, but he apparently cannot help it.

As soon as I told this story someone exclaimed: "Kohl (coal)!" I was under the impression that someone in the audience wanted in this way to characterize the color of the spot and I replied that it might be something else. Thereupon the man who had exclaimed arose and said: "But you are speaking of Mr. Kohl. I know him also!"

I did not of course have reference to this Mr. Kohl but to someone else. But this proof of the daily occurrence of such cases called forth great hilarity and at the same time offered an excellent means for bringing home to the parents, in an obvious manner, the importance of doing away with disciplinary education.

In conclusion I should like to point out another circumstance which is of great significance for the educational enlightenment offered to the parents at the meetings of the parents' associations. At these lectures the parents have a chance to show themselves in a different light owing to the absence of their children. Since they are not watched by their children, they lose nothing of their prestige—a state of mind from which most parents emancipate themselves only gradually, and some never. In this situation they do not mind being shown their mistakes and being advised, whereas in child guidance clinics where they have to bring their children along, they would remain deaf to any instruction. Such an unexpected change in the parents' attitude, which does not seem to have been provoked by any external conditions, has an excellent effect upon the children. They see in this a proof of the fact that the parents are actuated in their attitude toward them by spontaneous and sincere intentions independent of any outside influences. The educational effect of such a conviction is obvious.

TECHNIQUE OF EDUCATIONAL GUIDANCE

By Dr. Alexandra Adler

IN our guidance clinics we consider that to guide the parents is as important as to guide the children. In most cases we let in the parents before the children and try to obtain from them a detailed anamnesis. The child meanwhile remains in the hall where he entertains himself by playing with the other children who are also waiting for their turn to go in. It had been proposed by some guidance workers to let the child come in with the mother so as to enable the mother to state her complaint in the presence of the child. For it was believed that the privacy of the conversation would make the child who is distrustful from the very beginning more distrustful, and in this way contact would be rendered more difficult. To this we may object that complaints made in the presence of the child would only justify his distrust and we should thus gain nothing in the end. Provided the situation was handled tactfully, the order arrangement never gave rise to any difficulties. If the child by chance was on the point of crossing the threshold together with the mother, it was sufficient to address him in a friendly manner, to ask him, for instance, "You do not mind having your mother go in first, do you?" in order to secure his immediate consent.

Our problem is first to gain quickly an accurate picture of the child from the mother's narrative.

In the course of our practice we have gradually worked out a kind of scheme by which to question the parents. This scheme has finally been formulated in a detailed questionnaire which is used in the treatment of backward children. The Vienna section of the International Association for Individual Psychology has published this questionnaire, which is gladly used by beginners, and is quite popular in all guidance clinics. It contains the most important questions capable of throwing light upon the personality of the child and upon educational difficulties. The sequence and selection of questions are determined by the peculiar nature of each separate case.

It is advisable to ask first about the main difficulties which made the mother come to us. To be sure, we are quite well aware of the fact that in this way we get hold only of a symptom which does not contribute much to our understanding of the child. But we proceed in this manner, because we have in mind the psychology of the parents who nearly always regard the child from the point of view of these difficulties and who are therefore puzzled if we do not ask about them.

Our next step is to find out, since when have these difficulties been in existence. In most cases we can show that it was the emergence of a new situation that caused the change in the child's attitude. Of the three groups of children that are most seriously menaced with difficulties—namely, the pampered ones, the hated ones, and those afflicted with organ inferiority—it is the pampered ones who above all fail in new situations. It is almost obvious that a child whose wishes up to a certain time have been met half way, who has always been helped out, who has been spared all difficulties and unpleasant experiences—a child of whom nothing was demanded—it is obvious that such a child would get cold feet and give up the race as soon as he is confronted with a difficult situation.

This often takes place after the child enters school. He notices that the teacher and his comrades do not retreat before him or stoop to him, and he becomes perplexed. He has not been accustomed to have to court the favor of others; he naturally loses courage. He looks now for other means by which to awaken interest—a thing which he achieves easiest through disturbance, fighting, noise-making, etc. The child is then, as we are often told, "good at home but bad at school." He fails in his school work. Has he not been accustomed to find someone near him, ready to help him in any difficulty? Here at school he suddenly realizes that he is being left to his own resources; he is soon discouraged and consequently loses all interest.

Poor school work may of course be the result of inborn feeble-mindedness. But the percentage of cases presenting this trait is quite negligible in our work, simply because real feeble-mindedness is easily detected, and children afflicted with this are sent to special schools and institutions, so that their treatment does not concern us. If a certain case, however, suggests the possibility of feeble-mindedness, we set little store by intelligence tests. Our chief problem is then rather to find out whether the reactions of the child are "rational," that is to say, whether they take place with regard to a definite purpose, from the point of view of a guiding idea, of a life-style or life-plan,—no matter whether this purpose and idea are inside or outside the useful sphere of life. The feeble-minded one does not succeed in working out a life-plan, and in this way we cannot guess what he would do if he were to be placed in a new situation, since he lacks method in his procedures. If we have established that we have before us a really feeble-minded child, we must not forget that such a child, too, is amenable to educational influences, although he will prove less successful in the domain of intellectual work. Much more effort and time are, however, required for this treatment than for that of normal children. Besides, the parents often lose patience, believing that the child is just stupid. It is therefore advisable from the very beginning to entrust such a child, if not to a suitable institution, at least to one of our pedagogically trained assistants, who is willing to enter into relations with the parents and to occupy himself with the child several times a week.

A change of teachers may also prove disadvantageous to a child who has always been pampered and protected against difficulties, if the new teacher is more strict and is not so much interested in the child as the previous teacher. Very often educational difficulties start at the moment when a younger brother or sister is born into the family. In such a case the parents generally report of their own accord that the child has become quite jealous. The child feels that he has been dislodged from his sphere of influence, and he tries to meet the challenge with methods which soon lead him to the useless side of life. An analogous situation occurs in case a stepmother or stepfather comes into the house and jeopardizes his supremacy, naturally without any bad intention.

Such events form the most frequent immediate occasions for educational difficulties. When we have discovered these factors by means of proper questions, we are in a better position to understand the child. If the complaints of the parents show us that the child behaves as if he were in a hostile country, that he lies, fights, steals, that he is distrustful; we know that we are confronted with a hated or undesired child, or with one afflicted with organ inferiority. The former have experienced no love at home, and they thus are unsuccessful in their relations with the environment in their further life. Children with organ inferiorities who have not been given a compensation by means of a corresponding education expect from life nothing but difficulties, which they moreover exaggerate. (We should like, however, to point out that all these separate manifestations may occasionally show themselves among the most different types of backwardness, since the same effect may be produced by the most different constellations. Our classification into three main types of children was dictated by practical considerations, owing to the excessive accumulation of similar traits among these types).

Of greatest importance for our understanding of the child is finally the question of the order of a child's birth in the family. The unearthing of the significance of this fact is an achievement of Individual Psychology.

After we have obtained from the statements of the parents a clear picture of the child we have to consult the parents. And here everything depends on the tactfulness of our procedure. However bad the attitude of the parents may seem to us, we must not betray our indignation or resentment by even a single gesture. We must remember that parents are convinced of the correctness of their methods and that they ascribe the responsibility to heredity, lack of aptitude, school, and to external conditions. If we offend the parents by an abrupt remark, we have lost all hope of gaining their co-operation in our attempt to influence the child favorably, and we have made them our adversaries. They will repudiate the results of our first meeting and they will refuse to come a second time. We rather try to explain to the parents the faults of their children in a friendly and calm tone. It is advisable to select from the anamnesis certain facts as our starting point and to emphasize them strongly. Thus, in connection with a child that is afraid of being dominated by his brothers and sisters with whom he is at odds, we tell the mother that she is always right. "It is good," we say, "that you always take pains to show the children that you love all of them alike. You have probably noticed that the child suspects that the others are preferred to him, he is full of misgivings. The more you show the child that he is worth as much as the others, that you think of him as much as of the others, the more courageous will the child become—and this is the thing that matters most at present."

Or we say in regard to a mistaken educational policy used by the parents: "This might perhaps do in the case of other children. As far as this child is concerned, however, we should advise you perhaps to try the following method." And now we are able to suggest to the mother a mode of treatment which seems to us to be in accordance with the picture we have gained of the child. In this way we have succeeded, in almost all cases, in inducing the parents if not after the first, at least after the second, conversation, to change their previous tactics.

In our conversations with the parents we relentlessly try to make them realize that children must not be beaten. Beating can only lead to a discouragement of the child, and we know well enough that this can make the child worse and not better. In refutation of this maxim we often hear it said that numerous eminent men were beaten in their childhood. But the necessity of beating is certainly the last thing proved by such examples. These men attained eminence, not because of, but in spite of the beating.

The most frequent objection which parents make on this score is the following: "We have tried to be kind, we have tried to be severe, but our efforts have proved in vain." To this we say: "Just try perhaps to stick to a single method; if you have not succeeded so far, try to proceed as we advise you." We always dissuade parents from engaging in warfare with the child, since the child inevitably remains in the end the stronger party. This fact is also to be kept in mind in the all too frequent cases of eating difficulties, which occur almost exclusively in families where too great importance is in some way or other attached to eating. Nor would severity here lead us anywhere. The children to whom compulsory measures have been applied begin to vomit, to eat slowly, often taking hours for their meals. In such a case as well as in cases of similar habits we recommend to the parents to observe a policy of consistent passivity. The children who do not accomplish their purpose with their refusal to eat, soon give up their tactics. Wherever the nutritive condition of the child is such that there is risk of a too great diminution in the amount of food intake, even in a short time, it is advisable to leave inconspicuously in the room a dish with food which the child usually eats up between meals.

We cannot enter here upon all the small details of parents' guidance, we have to leave them to the art of the individual counsellors. The fundamental features of our method are always the same. It is our aim to make the parents our allies in order to train the children to become courageous and independent.

At the end of the first session we ask the parents to continue coming to the clinic for a time; we then take leave of them and let the child come in. The parents leave the room.

We are often asked whether it is a sensible policy to deal with a child in the presence of other people. In our own ranks, too, there were at the beginning some skeptics in regard to this point.

Our own experience extending over a long period justifies us, however, in advocating complete publicity of treatments. (It is always a question here of children of school age. In marginal cases we vary our policy according to circumstances). We have already dealt with this question in the article. Here we should only like to point out that continuous observations have shown us that children are much less embarrassed by publicity than adults, and that their slight embarrassments completely disappear after a few seconds if we assume the proper tone. Our purpose is above all justified by the fact—and this is our most important point of view—that the child notices that his case has a social connection. It is to this aspect that his attention is turned by publicity—a method the importance of which follows from the fundamental tenets of Individual Psychology.

It may happen sometimes that the child does not speak at all at the beginning. In such a case we alone speak to the child; we speak about things which presumably may interest the child and which may fall upon fertile soil. We are mainly concerned at first with gaining the sympathy of the child. We therefore start quite often with apparently different things, and we continue talking in such a vein until a sudden flash in his eyes tells us that a contact has been established with him. As soon as the child notices that it is not a question here of an arraignment, his favor has been won.

Now we are prepared to take up the study of the situation of the child in a more detailed manner. It is only seldom, and this in the case of older children,—that is to say, of those that are about twelve years old,—that it is advisable to reveal to them their whole situation, their mistakes and false aims. In this respect the treatment of children differs from that of adults. What forms the goal of our treatment in the case of adults is for obvious reasons out of place and also impossible in the case of children. We confine ourselves here to occasional brief explanations of the difficulties with which the child is handicapped. We would, for instance, say to a pampered child who does not get ahead at school: "You have believed that everything goes by itself, and because you have difficulties with your school work, you believe that you cannot succeed in anything and you give up the race."

Further and deeper explanations would be beyond the reach of the child.

We have won our game if we have succeeded in encouraging the child in some way or other. To be sure our starting point cannot be arbitrary. We must begin at the source of his errors. Since we aim above all to stimulate self-confidence and self-respect, we gladly attach ourselves to some positive achievement of the child. Thus we ask a backward child who likes to draw to bring us a drawing the next time. We are always astonished to see how gladly and punctually the children fulfill their task, how much joy our interest gives them, and how proud they are of our praise. After he has shown us the drawing, we tell him that he certainly could write equally well if he were willing to practice in writing as much as in drawing. We later have him bring some of his written work, pointing out to him even the smallest progress made. This method has proved to be quite successful.

It is well known that pampered children always rely upon others, and have their parents dress them, feed them, etc. We endeavor to bring home to such a child that it would be good for him to try to dress by himself, assuring him that he certainly is able to do what other children can do. We also tell him that we understand quite well why so far he has not dressed himself, but that now since he is getting older, things will be different. Through this we facilitate matters for the child, since he then considers the change as natural and he does not feel any longer that he is giving up an important position. In this way we gradually increase the independence of the child. It is precisely this that shows the importance of winning over the parents as our allies, for in this stimulation to independence they suspect a kind of attempt to detach the child from their influence—a thing which they do not always regard favorably in the beginning.

If the child has already selected a vocation—this is always a good omen—we can utilize this circumstance quite profitably. I have to think here of the case of an intelligent boy of eleven years who firmly made up his mind to become an architect. He used to draw well and to make pretty constructions. He was somewhat crippled and a so-called bad child—he felt that he was always victimized. He fought with the other children, and made himself unpopular. We spoke to him about his future calling and told him that we regard him, on the basis of the work he has done so far, as especially qualified for it. We also pointed out to him how necessary it will be for him as an architect to co-operate in a friendly manner with the people surrounding him, and how little people would esteem an architect who engages in fist-fights with his workers whenever anything displeases him. The boy laughed, he was won for us. It is true that in this way we have awakened his ambition, but it was an ambition directed towards the useful side of life.

As can be seen from this example, we always endeavor to stimulate in the child both courage and a capacity for human contact. We also try to show him that to be in constant conflict with everyone means to remain always the weaker party.

In child guidance, just as well as in parents' guidance, we do not wish to lay down a final scheme that works for all cases. It is the fundamental principles of Individual Psychology which suggest the proper means and devices in the course of the conversation with the child. It is from them that we have derived the ideas of the present article. The technique of educational guidance is on the whole the same in all our guidance clinics and is undergoing few changes of late. In this we have had no predecessors. It is therefore the result of a development which we owe to our own experience, to our practical participation in the work of the educational guidance clinics for Individual Psychology.

ERRORS IN THE TECHNIQUE OF GUIDANCE WORK

By Dr. Alexander Müller

THE task of the guidance worker is beset with many difficulties. Home conditions, the situation of the child at school, may be of such a nature and may offer such resistance to the influence of the guidance worker as to render the transformation of the child not only difficult but even impossible. There are, moreover, other obstacles of what we should call an objective nature which frustrate the work of the guidance worker. But apart from objective obstacles, failures are often due to the method used by the guidance worker. Even if he is completely equipped with theoretical knowledge, he may still fail; he may fail whenever he has sufficient knowledge but not sufficient art. He cannot be said to have accomplished much if he has merely discovered the false life-plan and the cause of backwardness, nor even if he has succeeded in showing the road that leads to the proper goal. To achieve real success he must possess the ability, yes, the art, of making the parents and the child follow the road which he has found to be the right one.

These subjective obstacles to the success of guidance work are accordingly errors of a technical nature, and we shall discuss here those that are most important practically.

One of the demands which Individual Psychology makes most strongly upon psychotherapists is to disregard their own interests completely. This has even more justification in the case of the guidance worker. For it is only through an impersonal attitude that he can arouse in the parents and the child the feeling that everything is done here with a view to their good and to that of the good cause. If he succeeds by his attitude in making them feel that he plays the impersonal part of a representative of society and of an interpreter of the ways recognized and sanctioned by it, it will be easy for him to convince them of the correctness of his views and proposals. Accordingly, the more the guidance worker is convinced of the correctness of the conceptions and methods of Individual Psychology, the more convincing will his activity be. He will not only strike at the proper moment upon the right thing for convincing the people that come for advice, he will also be able to stand opposition. The more certain he is of his cause, the less it is a question for him of personal success, that is, the easier it will be for him to act in an unbiassed manner. Thus, one's own conviction and an impersonal attitude run parallel to and support one another. It is obvious that these qualities are present to a smaller extent in younger and less experienced guidance workers than in more experienced ones. Guidance workers with little practical experience crave for activity too much, they are still too much interested in success, and their whole behavior is hardly of a nature to arouse in the people coming for advice the feeling that it is questions of solid truths which are not to be shaken through personal conflicts. But it is also evident that he must not state these truths too apodictically, that he must again and again emphasize the fact that they are matters of common experience, and that he is proposing them in the present case only for trial; in general he must not arouse in his listeners the spirit of contradiction.

There is one dangerous obstacle in the way of the guidance worker. He has to perform two services which mothers are supposed to render to their children. Most mothers fulfill the first task properly, that is, they allow the child to be a reliable person and give him the opportunity, by living with him, to experience what it means to be such a person. They, however, often neglect their second task: they fail to detach the child from themselves and to initiate him into social life, by encouraging him, by training him to be independent, by fostering in him an ability for making contacts. The guidance worker, too, often runs the risk of committing the same error. In the desire to win the favorable disposition of the child, to be attentive to him, to be sympathetic to his wishes, many a guidance worker overshoots the mark and spoils the child in the end. He may be successful insofar as he makes the child give up some of his bad habits or errors for his, the guidance worker's, sake. The child may even give the appearance of considerable improvement, but there can hardly be a question in such a case of real change of life-plan. And this must form the goal of guidance work.

Nor is this task fulfilled by guidance workers in cases where the situation of the child appears to them to be so difficult that they apply their efforts only to make things easier for him, without curing the disease. However justified such a desire may be, we cannot say that we have done much so long as we have not changed the child. We must aim to train the child so as to enable him to cope by himself with difficult situations.

In this connection we should also like to point out that encouragement alone is not sufficient. We may often succeed, by means of a proper technique, in encouraging the child and in bringing him for a time to the right path. But as long as we have not discovered his erroneous life-plan and as long as we have not enabled him to get a proper insight into connections, the success is only apparent and the false life-plan will come again to light whenever corresponding difficulties present themselves.

One of the clearest and most unambiguous demands of Individual Psychology is to pay less attention to the separate symptoms of every parent and child and to deal rather with the personality as a whole. This demand is often not sufficiently complied with. Led by the desire to offer quick help to impatient parents and to remove as soon as possible the disturbing errors in the case of specially difficult children, many of the less experienced guidance workers readily turn their attention to these aspects. The result is that they do not see the wood for the trees. It is quite possible for numerous symptoms to be made to disappear in this way. But this does not mean that new bad habits may not come up again in the place of the old ones. In such a case we have to say again that the work has not been done completely, and that the changing of the life-plan has thus been neglected. One of the most frequent technical errors in guidance work is, unfortunately, this method of treating symptoms instead of dealing with the child as a whole and transforming the whole personality.

Guidance workers finally may not be completely successful because they deal with the people coming to them for advice in too dry and theoretical manner. We may grasp the situation properly enough, we may also give the right advice, but we shall nevertheless fail when we are unable to carry on the conversation with the child and parents in a vivid and dramatic manner. In order to impress the child and to be able to help him, we must in our conversation set his soul in sympathetic vibration. To shape a conversation vividly and not merely to impart to others dry and grey truths in a bloodless fashion, is undoubtedly in a certain sense an artistic accomplishment, which we have a chance to practice in daily life. If we wish to help and sustain someone as a fellow being, we shall easily find the right ways and means by identifying ourselves into his situation, by identifying ourselves with him. We may say that this ability for identifying oneself into the situation of another person is the condition for understanding, and accordingly for guiding, our fellow beings. This identification at the same time prevents us from theorizing too much. It will also enable us to act in the right manner: not to make pontifical pronouncements, not to play the judge, not to be condescending, or obtrusive, but to be reserved and also unyielding when necessary.

Identification is of the greatest importance

for the guidance worker. The ability to identify himself with the situation of the people coming to him for advice, is alone sufficient to warrant success. One whose social sympathies are so wide that he is able to identify himself with his fellow beings, will also be able to strike the right tone whenever he is dealing with them, to get the proper insight into their lives, and to help them in a successful way.

A CASE FROM GUIDANCE PRACTICE

By Dr. Alfred Adler

FRITZ, twelve years old, was introduced to our child guidance clinic on the twenty-first of November, in the company of his mother. Dr. Marianne Langer gave an introductory report. The report and explanatory remarks made by the adviser are reproduced here in small type in accordance with the stenographic text:

Fritz, twelve years old, comes into the clinic suffering from enuresis.

He is a militant child, was probably pampered in his early childhood, but was thrown out of this pampered position by some event or other. He does not feel well at present and begins to make such demands on his mother that she also has to attend to him during the night, We must look here for signs of his previous pampered state: that he is slovenly as a rule, probably jealous of a younger or older sister or brother, has difficulties with eating, and wants to be in the center of things and to draw others near himself.

. . . frequently during the day . . .

When we hear that a child wets himself we can infer that it is a case of violent struggle. He is not satisfied with bothering others at night, he does it also during the day. We have also to ascertain whether we are not confronted here with a mental defect. Organic diseases occur seldom in these cases.

. . . seldom at night.

While struggling violently during the day, he seems to be in a better situation at night, when he quiets down. We shall not be surprised to learn that he carries on his struggle consciously, and that defiance is an outstanding feature of his character. Defiance is a somewhat more conscious struggle.

He never wets himself when his mother is with him or when he is at school.

This shows that we have to deal with psychic motives. When his mother is with him there is no necessity for drawing her near him. At school he probably does not feel bad either. He may not be a bad pupil at all, or perhaps he does not like the idea of being thrown out of school.

The mother is separated . . .

Matrimonial discords have a bad effect upon children. When parents quarrel, they often give vent to their ill-humor in the presence of their children. It is a striking fact that backward, delinquent, neurotic, sexually perverse, drinking children very often come from families with unhappy matrimonial relations. It is important to find out whether the child is not overburdened; overburdening is always a cause of difficulties.

. . . he lives with his grandparents . . .

Here we must remember that grandparents generally pamper children. To be sure, not always: if the mother does the pampering, then she is blamed by the grandmother; if the mother does not pamper, then the grandmother does the pampering.

The child used to sleep in the parents' bedroom.

This shows either that the pampered child himself made efforts to be with his parents or that the parents always wanted to keep him near themselves.

At present he sleeps alone.

This circumstance cannot be indifferent to us, it plays a part in the enuresis. If the child slept in the mother's bed, he would not wet himself.

The child is tremendously attached to his mother . . .

This confirms our supposition that the bond between the mother and the child is a very intimate one. He tries to gain the mother for himself and to use her as a prop.

He is especially pampered by his grandmother.

We see then that we did not go far astray in our suppositions.

Four years ago he was laid up for seven weeks in the hospital with osteomyelitis of the hip and thigh.

This is an ailment which is extraordinarily favorable to pampering. After such an ailment children feel the need of pampering more intensely.

It looked at that time as if the leg would have to be amputated, but it was healed through ancylotic treatment.

In other words we have to deal with a bodily defect—a circumstance that largely contributes to developing a feeling of inferiority in the child. The mere fact that children are pampered is sufficient to generate in them a feeling of inferiority and to deprive them of self-confidence. The treatment by ancylosis tends to intensify this feeling of inferiority and makes the patient rely a great deal upon the support of others.

On account of this disease he did not attend school from the age of seven to ten.

It is obvious that he was always in the company of his mother.

At the age of ten he was put in the third class of the school for backward children and he is at present in the fourth class of this school.

To attend a school for backward children means an intensification of the feeling of inferiority if the child is not an imbecile or an idiot. If the child is feeble-minded, he is naturally not aware of the fact that he is exclusively among backward children. A normal child, on the other hand, feels that he is being degraded if he is sent to such a school. Such a child has many reasons to think that he is inferior and degraded.

He gets ahead in school quite well.

If he is normal it is not surprising to see him

get ahead. There is no advantage in this for him. To see with one eye among the totally blind is no triumph.

He has some difficulties with arithmetic.

If he is only shown properly how to do the thing, he will certainly be able to calculate just as well as the others.

When one of the pupils is asked a question in school he always butts in with his answers.

This suggests that he is an intelligent boy. This pampered child would like to stand in the foreground. His wetting of the bed is also a means to this end. He plays quite a good role at school, he is probably not entirely dissatisfied, but he would like to be prominent, and this is why he butts in with his answers.

In playing, also, he must always play the first fiddle.

He has his *style-of-life*—a thing not to be found among feeble-minded children. We can say that the school for backward childen is not a place for him. We know that he is not prepared for a normal class as a result of his diseases, and that he could not make much progress there without preparation. It would be necessary to establish a special preparatory school for such children.

He has a brother who is four years older than he and who also has been greatly pampered by his father.

We can infer from this that he has no younger brothers or sisters. He probably goes around with the idea that his elder brother is, in comparison with him, quite favored by fortune. The latter is preferred by the father and he does not have to go to the school for backward children.

The elder brother is very handsome, was left back once, but he is quite a good pupil now. He is very serious and grown-up.

If the elder brother is well-developed and is not to be beaten, then the younger one becomes the chief problem. If the younger one makes good progress, keeps up with his brother and threatens his supremacy, then the elder one becomes a problem. This experience is confirmed in the present case. The elder brother probably does not lose an opportunity to point out that the younger one is in a school for backward children.

The younger gladly plays the clown.

This happens frequently in the case of children who have a feeling of inferiority and who try to push themselves to the foreground. We find in this child three co-ordinated facts: enuresis, the tendency to butt in with his answers when others are questioned, and to play the clown. These are nothing but forms of expression chosen by ambitious weaklings. Anyone with a feeling of self-confidence would not act in this way.

He often cries out at night.

Here again, he looks for attention. That he cries out, that he plays the clown, shows that he is intelligent, that he proceeds in the right way, that he does things in the same way as we would do, if I may say so, if we were in the same position.

With eating he has no difficulties.

A sign that no great errors have been committed by the family in this regard is the fact that the importance of eating is not unduly stressed. The child has started off wrong in his development, and we should really expect him to have difficulties with eating. We must not be surprised at the fact that we fail to observe in the structure of a *style-of-life,* things which we might reasonably expect on the basis of our experience with the general run of such cases.

He washes and dresses by himself.

In this respect, too, the family has evidently proceeded in the right way.

The parents and the paternal grandparents are blood-relations.

This would properly speaking be of no significance, for the facts observed in this case can also be found in other children. The difficulties cannot be reduced here to heredity. But I should like to point out that I always find marriages between blood-relations among discouraged persons; such persons look for a sort of security in the selection of their life mates, and they find this in persons whom they have known since their childhood. This also bears testimony to a poorly developed social sentiment, because all society is confined for these people to the family. It must not be denied that the offspring of blood-relations may often display organ inferiorities (defects of ears or eyes). But as far as I have been able to establish this is only true in cases where both partners happen to possess parallel inferiorities. We very often see quite healthy children in families with no parallel inferiorities. We are opposed to marriages between blood-relations simply because the proper development of the social sentiment requires the widest blood-mixture possible. People who discriminate so greatly between persons of their own family and those of others do not possess much of this sentiment.

The child had whooping-cough and bladder trouble.

These ailments offer another occasion for great pampering. We may observe that there are a number of diseases, such as scarlet fever, whooping-cough, and encephalitis, which inevitably entail pampering. Numerous subsequent difficulties can be reduced to these diseases. Sometimes we may notice that a difficult child improves after a serious disease. It would, however, be hardly true to maintain that scarlet fever may have a favorable effect upon anyone.

He began to walk at the age of sixteen months.

If we were to believe the mother, the disease

of rickets was perhaps partly responsible for the trouble. It is evident that he was under the care of his mother more than was necessary.

He did not learn to speak until he was three.

This shows that he had no great need of speaking. Had he had such a need, he would have spoken earlier. All his wishes were fulfilled, everything was done for him so that there was no necessity for him to speak. This also happens in the case of the deaf-mute. Such children are generally pampered to an extraordinary extent and they thus have no necessity for speaking. Mothers often remark with pride that they always know what the child wants. Such children always wish to be understood without speaking and to be constantly attended to. If such a child does not speak and if the pampering person satisfies all his whims, we can naturally expect to have on our hands a deaf-mute. We also know that children can form and regulate all their functions in accordance with their environment.

I once heard of a child of a deaf-mute couple. This child was quite normal, he was able to hear and speak. Whenever he hurt himself he used to cry out loud. Tears ran down his cheeks and he made a sad face, but did not cry out loud; he knew that it would have been useless. The functions grow in accordance with the environment —they cannot grow otherwise. Here we can call upon the psychology of instincts. The development of instincts is a function of the environment. The child in this case was spared the necessity of speaking; his speech, therefore, had no chance to develop at the proper time.

Even now he speaks somewhat nasally. He was operated on four years ago for tonsils and adenoids. He has soon to undergo another operation for adenoids. He is somewhat of a mongoloid type.

It is somewhat stunning to hear that he is of a mongoloid type, for this involves a suspicion that he belongs to the class of feeble-minded children. I should not, however, be inclined to make such a deduction from the mere fact that he is mongoloid.

The upper part of his nose is wide, his ears stand out, the lower lip protrudes; otherwise internal nerve conditions are normal. Intelligence normal. His right leg is stiff. He takes great delight in athletic sports, and although this was at first forbidden him, he managed, as far as his leg permitted, to participate in them.

I have often noticed that children with defective arms or legs take part with great zeal in athletic sports and sometimes become very successful. Here we find another confirmation for one of the fundamental views of Individual Psychology. The best accomplishments are made possible by a special interest entailed by an organ inferiority.

Within the short time given to us we cannot achieve everything we could and should like to achieve. If some one could be put at the disposal of the mother and child, our work would yield richer results. Our immediate task is to make the child courageous and independent, to offer him special tutoring so as to enable him to go back to his normal school. He is to be provided with an end in view, which will show him how to achieve something splendid on the useful side of life; and in proportion as he succeeds, his bad qualities will lose all value for him. To wet himself is his last refuge. We shall show him a better way.

We must also win the favor of the mother. For if we make such a proposal to the child and the mother works against us, the child will become involved in difficulties. I shall now show the mother the true nature of the child and shall try to influence her accordingly.

(The mother is called in.)

Adler (to the mother): I wish to speak about your Fritz. Is he not one of the best pupils of his class?

Mother: I could not say that.

Adler: Is he not one of the best pupils in the school for backward children?

Mother: Everything is all right except arithmetic. Other children are ahead of him. The teacher says that when he reads quietly he does well. He tries to go too fast.

Adler: What would he like to become?

Mother: A cabinet-maker.

Adler: What does his father do?

Mother (with pride): He is a dental mechanic. The grandfather has a furniture business. My father says he would like Fritz to learn the trade in order that he may understand the furniture business.

Adler: He means that he should become a cabinet-maker. Does he have any friends?

Mother: Yes, but younger children exclusively.

Adler: Has he any inclination to be with other children?

Mother: He wants to play with smaller children only.

Adler: Has he ever been sent to a guidance clinic?

Mother: He was with the "Friends of Children." The children once had a quarrel, and the teacher gave them a sound thrashing.

Adler: Does he tell the truth?

Mother: He sometimes makes up stories, but he does not lie.

Adler: Does he know how to go about with money?

Mother: Yes, he knows how to go about with money.

Adler: Is he reliable?

Mother: Yes, he is very reliable. He makes himself useful in the business. He knows very well what he is doing, takes care of the telephone and attends to matters quite well. Only he is too childish.

Adler: How does he feel at school?

Mother: He feels quite well at school. We had sent him, for a time, to a private school; we hoped that it would be easier for him there. But not much attention was paid to him there and he was allowed to be left back. A nerve specialist, a friend of ours, found the child to be normal and advised us to send him to the school for backward children.

Adler: How are the children in the school for backward children?

Mother: The children are terrible, but this does not worry him. There are horrible children there who are very backward. If I knew positively that I can expect him to forge ahead. . . .

Adler: But you have never doubted that?

Mother: The teachers always consoled me with the thought that he will be a good business man. He is interested in all kinds of things, has an opinion of his own about many matters and gives the impression of a good deal of independence. If only it were not for his childishness. . . .

Adler: Does he often wet himself?

Mother: I also went to see his teacher and asked her how things are with him at school. She complains that he wets himself in school, too.

She says it must be a weakness. Of late things have again become worse.

Adler: Has he gotten worse at school?

Mother: He gets ahead. Formerly he was unable to do his school work by himself, but at present he does it quite independently.

Adler: Has he not been scolded? What about his arithmetic?

Mother: In arithmetic other children are ahead of him.

Adler: It would be well if he could get ahead in arithmetic also. Would you like to send him to our guidance clinic? Can he travel by himself?

Mother: He travels entirely by himself. He also travels to school by himself.

Adler: It will be brought home to him at the clinic that he can attain everything and that he can go back to the regular school.

Mother: When he was with the "Friends of Children" he made beautiful things. Once he constructed a pretty theatre. To believe his teacher, he has something in him that no child has,—he is very conscientious.

Adler: It would be much better for the boy to go back to the regular school. How is the other boy?

Mother: A splendid lad.

Adler: What is his attitude towards the younger brother?

Mother: They like each other immensely. At present the situation is quite different. I live with my parents, the older boy is with the other grandmother, and the children do not see each other so often.

Adler: Does he tease the younger brother?

Mother: He sympathizes greatly with him and trembles for him.

Adler: He behaves like a father. This is very often found in the case of victorious elder brothers.

Mother: The elder one was always very well developed.

Adler: The elder one seems to be very popular.

Mother: The younger one is still more so. The elder one has a proud character.

Adler: Has he not been teased or ridiculed on

account of the school for backward children?

Mother: He is not teased on account of the school, but the children tease and ridicule him on account of his leg—it is terrible!

Adler: This will stop eventually. His habit of wetting himself will also stop. I should like to advise you to *encourage* the child, not to criticize him, not to scold him, but to stimulate him to do everything by himself.

Mother: My family criticizes and continually finds fault with him.

Adler: Tell them in my name to hold back their scolding, criticizing, and nagging. We shall apply a new method and change him for the better.

Mother takes leave, with thanks.

Adler: That he is always provoked at home is of great importance. I don't know whether you have ever seen the tapir in the Schönbrunner zoological garden. This tapir has the habit of turning around and urinating whenever he is annoyed or irritated by someone; it is highly unpleasant, sometimes he vents his anger upon an entirely innocent victim.

(The child enters the room.)

Adler (to the child): How do you get along at school?

Fritz: Well.

Adler: You are quite a clever boy. You could be quite a proficient pupil. I believe you are cowardly, you have no confidence in yourself. You believe that this stuff, this arithmetic, is too much for you. You will manage it easily, I will see to it that you become good at figuring! . . . We could then arrange matters so as to enable you to go to a higher school. I shall help you there also. We shall take matters promptly into our own hands, and suddenly you will discover that things move ahead. I should like you to come to our center where you can play and do your school work also. You will have a good time there. . . . I was also poor in arithmetic, then someone showed me how to do it, and I became the best pupil in arithmetic. What would your teacher think if you became the best pupil in arithmetic?

Fritz: It would give her pleasure.

Adler: Would you like to give her pleasure?

Fritz: Yes!

Adler: Come again soon and don't mind if a boy tells you something silly. You know that they say these things out of sheer stupidity. And when you are criticized at home, you must not get angry at once either, and make yourself wet. You must help me! May I rely upon you? (Takes leave of the child.)

ON EDUCATIONAL METHODS WHICH ARE BASED UPON INDIVIDUAL PSYCHOLOGY

(A dialogue between an educational guidance worker for Individual Psychology and a physician.)

By Martha Holub *and* Dr. Alexander Neuer

H.: I often marvel at the apparent success achieved by child guidance clinics that are directed by non-adherents of Individual Psychology. Don't you always maintain that academic psychologists as well as psycho-analysts are naturalists and that naturalists are in reality logically committed to a therapeutic and logical nihilism?

N.: This can be readily explained. All these people who repudiate Individual Psychology have two souls in their breast. They represent a personal union between science and man. As scientists who especially lay pompous claims to the exactness of the natural sciences they are indeed committed to the passivity of man, since every active interference with nature is for natural science an inexplicable miracle. As persons, however, confronted with the duties of the educator and therapist, they give reality to this miracle every minute of the day, by throwing a veil over their logical inconsistency and by imperceptibly rendering help with methods dictated to them by their practical knowledge of human nature.

H.: You seem thus to believe, doctor, that it is sufficient to be a man among men in order to act in accordance with the principles which we, followers of Individual Psychology, regard as the principles of our science.

N.: Yes, this is exactly my opinion. We must not imagine that prior to 1907 humanity did not proceed therapeutically or pedagogically. But just as there is a difference between the pre-scientific physics of primitive peoples and laymen and the scientific physics since Galileo and Newton, so there is also a difference between the pre-scientific treatment of children and disease and scientific Individual Psychology since Alfred Adler. In all these cases it is a question of the egg of Columbus which was then regarded by humanity as the achievement of a genius.

H.: I shall illustrate your opinion about the incongruity between the theory and practice of the non-adherents of Individual Psychology by means of references taken from psycho-analytic literature. In the preface to the highly readable book of the psycho-analyst August Aichhorn, Freud expresses the view that psycho-analysis and education are not the same thing and that psycho-analysis is to be applied in special cases only and that it by no means forms a presupposition for education!

"The possibility of exercising an analytic influence rests upon certain definite presuppositions, which can be summed up as the 'analytic situation'; it requires the development of certain psychic structures, a special attitude towards the analyst. Whenever these are absent, as is the case with children, with youthful delinquents, and as a rule with instinctive criminals, we have to resort to something else rather than to analysis."

And Anna Freud writes in the same way in her introduction to the technique of child analysis:

"I expect certain practical analysts among

you to say that the opinions uttered here show that what I do with children has, despite all these differences, not much to do with real analysis. It may be said that what I use is a 'wild method' [and therefore a human one—Remark of the lecturer] which borrows everything from analysis without doing justice to strict analytic rules. If in your office hours there came to you for treatment a grown-up neurotic who upon closer inspection should prove to be so instinctive, so undeveloped intellectually, so largely dependent upon his environment as is the case with my child patients, you would probably then say: The Freudian analysis is an excellent method, but it is not meant for such people. And you would then treat the patient in a mixed manner, you would give him as much of pure analysis as is compatible with his character, and the rest would consist of child analysis, because infantile as his whole character is, he deserves nothing better."

N.: Your quotations after all bear testimony to the scientific conscience which separates psycho-analysis from education. Aichhorn himself does this explicitly when he says in the book you mentioned that in cases of pronounced delinquency psycho-analysis accomplishes nothing, education everything. You can see that Aichhorn is an intuitive educator and a student of human nature, that he is, so to speak, an Individual Psychologist by avocation, and that he utilizes psycho-analysis only as an apparent theoretical justification for his activity. Much more consistent is the position of Siegfried Bernfeld who designates the work of education as a Sisyphean task "exactly because psycho-analysis is a natural science, and therefore indifferent to values," and pedagogy cannot make a single step without purposes and values. It is necessary to illustrate this discrepancy between theory and practice by concrete examples.

H.: In this respect I can be of some help. I could show you that psycho-analysis was unessential, that the treatment was on the basis of Individual Psychology in all the cases of Aichhorn's book which were treated successfully. The same is true of Anna Freud wherever she does not stick strictly to the laws of her doctrine and makes room instead for "human efforts and influences." We see, for instance, how Aichhorn at first tries to restore "feeling contact" then unearths the strong side—in this case music—so as to enhance the youth's feeling of self-confidence. But in proceeding in this way Aichhorn certainly acts in the spirit of Individual Psychology, even though the theoretical interpretation is given here in terms of psycho-analysis, asserting that the father is the object of love and at the same time a rival for the stepmother's love.

N.: I can assure you that most of the terms used in psycho-analysis are nothing but circumscriptions for the customary relations among human beings and that the underlying idea even of the famous Œdipus complex is not the mystic and mythically mysterious sexual wishes of children, but the eternal struggle of the oppressed against their oppressors. Aichhorn, too, represents his ideas in a similar manner. He points out that he exercises his influence upon delinquents by approaching them not as an adult, not as an authority bent upon combatting them, but as a sympathetic ally. I wonder how Aichhorn manages without "libidinous relations," since in dealing with the difficulties confronting the attempts at influencing mothers he regards pampering only as the cause of dissociality. I should like to reproduce the following case in detail:

A public school pupil, a girl of thirteen, appears with her foster-mother in the guidance clinic. According to complaint, the girl is defiant, unpunctual, unreliable, given to lying, reluctant to do any housework. It is a question here of an only child, who grew up in the country, has lost her parents and is at present in the house of Viennese relatives. The transplantation into a different environment, so writes Aichhorn, means an uncommonly great hardship for an only child who formerly occupied a privileged position in the house of her parents. At present she feels that she is only being tolerated, and that she is only a nurse-maid for her cousin who is three and a half years old.

Despite the psycho-analytic explanations which Aichhorn gives for the conflict in the child's soul, he also points out that the only proper and therapeutically effective way of dealing with the situation is to put the child in an environment favorably disposed to her. But this certainly is the method of Individual Psychology.

N.: I can imagine that academic psychologists and psycho-analysts intend the application of their psychology not so much for the child as for themselves. The psychologist who knows the laws of thought, feeling, and volition, will, on the basis of these laws, discover the best method for himself in order to realize best an educational ideal lying outside psychology. The psycho-analyst familiar with the sadism and mania for authority of adults will hope that by analyzing the educator he will cure him of these qualities which are not favorable to education. To this it might be objected that a physician may, on the basis of his knowledge, in a special pathological case forbid a patient the use of alcohol and nicotin without having to become himself abstinent. It may be also granted, on the other hand, that only a good person will be a good educator. But how in the world can academic psychology and psycho-analysis make any one a good person? There is an enormous gulf between the world of facts and the world of the ideals according to which we aim to bring up the younger generation. Individual Psychology tries by means of its therapy of encouragement to free the individual from the clutches of neurotic pretexts and to stimulate in him a feeling of responsibility. This can happen only in case the individual is conscious of his duties towards society. The ideal of our education is both negative and positive: Don't be a quitter, fulfill your obligations towards your social environment, towards your fellow beings, in your vocation and in marriage. It is only an axiological psychology, that is, a psychology which, unlike the natural sciences, is not indifferent to value, that is able to supply the educator and the therapist with the proper instruments. It is only a psychology based upon values that can avoid the logical inconsistencies and subterfuges which are so current in all the pedagogical and therapeutical methods used by non-individual psychology. Every step leads in logical purity from the theory to the practice of Individual Psychology.

SMALL CHILDREN IN GUIDANCE CLINICS

By Ida Loewy

IF a small child is brought to our guidance clinics with educational difficulties, it is advisable to impress the parents or educators with the importance of the fact that to be grown-up is for small children the ideal of everything they can and are allowed to do,—the goal of all their aspirations. Nothing can be so conducive to education as to allow such children to do what they wish, provided they do not harm themselves or others. We are all familiar with the beaming faces which children have whenever they are allowed, for instance, to hold tickets in street cars. We have to realize that for children everything is an accomplishment, a proof of their abilities, of their value; that everything shows them how near they come to us adults and how independent they become of us.

If a small child presents any difficulties in training we shall generally accomplish much more by speaking to him about what he can do than by pointing out to him his failures. This is true of the conversation of the parents with the child as well as of that of the guidance worker. In this way the child learns to realize that he already understands and can do all kinds of difficult things, and that it is not necessary for him to be so silly at a time when much smaller children act sensibly.

A method specially suitable to the educational guidance of small children and to their training in general is to strengthen their consciousness of self-worth in an indirect manner. For this purpose it is advisable to say something good about the child to his parents or educators when he is within hearing distance. The child listens with great interest when he hears his name. He acquiesces in the consciousness of being appreciated, and the realization that he can do things often leads to an improvement of his behavior.

I shall give here two small examples to show how effectively children can be influenced by this indirect method. In both cases I was supported sympathetically by the mother, whom I had informed beforehand about my intentions.

Case I. Liesl was an only child, two years old, constantly kept her mother busy, did not want to play by herself for a moment, got furious if the mother even wanted to read a letter, used to burst out crying whenever she was taken to bed, was unfriendly to other children. When the child, who was attended to in the clinic by a bigger child, came within hearing distance, I asked the mother: "Does Liesl also have a friend just like big children?" The mother answered: "Yes, she too will soon have a friend." I said: "You will soon be able to go to kindergarten where you will find many children to play and sing with." And I continued: "Does Liesl also go to bed by herself like big children?"

This conversation took place in the afternoon. I had asked the mother not to speak about it any more to the child, in order to see whether anything would stick to her. The next day I learned that nothing had been said to her about it and the parents felt that she had forgotten all about it. In the evening, however, she made no fuss when going to bed, often repeating: "Aunt say, children sleep—friend." The child's mind was no longer moving within a world where orders are taken, and obedience is denied, but within a world where achievements are possible.

Case II. Erna is two years and three months old; she has a younger brother who is six weeks old. She was regarded as extremely bad: she never did what she was asked to do; quite often she threw out of the window everything that came into her hands; she was insolent, she said, for instance, to a lady who came to visit her mother: "You stupid woman!" and nearly always vomited when her mother wanted to go out.

I had asked the mother to remain calm, however strange the things I said or did to the child might appear to her; I would give her all the necessary explanations afterwards. I had put my hand-bag on the table, the child tried to grasp it, and I said: "I shall show you how to open it." She, indeed, could not know how to operate the peculiar mechanism of the bag. I continued: "You would now like to see what is in it; you may take out everything if you wish, except my purse and the notes that are in it." She took out everything, but left the purse and the notes inside. She began to play with my flash-light. With the words, "Now you will see something pretty!" I lighted the flash-light and let her do the same several times. Then I put my thumb imperceptibly upon the mechanism and said: "We'll let it go for today, we shall do it again tomorrow." Without wincing she dropped this and turned to other things. While I began to speak to her mother, she crumpled up a sheet of drawing-paper and put it into her mouth. I got up quickly and sat down before her little brother, and said to her: "I don't like little Fritz to see you doing such things." At this moment her father entered and the child calmly left the room with him.

After a while she came back, opened her mouth in order to show me that it was empty. Presently she stood up on her toes, began to clap hands, and, giving me a penetrating glance, she said: "Lion." The mother said quietly to me: "Now you will hear some music." The child continued: "Camel, elephant." I asked her: "What other animals do you know? Dog, cat, horse?" The child turned aside. Meanwhile the little brother woke up. I looked at him and spoke to the mother. The girl, who wanted to attract my attention, again put paper in her mouth and came up to me. But I did not look at her and said: "Excuse me, I am now speaking to Fritz." She rapidly took the paper out of her mouth, threw it aside, and showed me that her mouth was again empty. After some time she came up to me and said just as she did before: "Old, old witch." I replied: "Please speak very low, I should not like Fritz to hear such things." The girl stood up on her toes and prepared to say something in my ear, but suddenly she stopped. After a few moments in which she tried to come back to herself, she whispered: "Trude"—the name of her friend, as her mother told me later.

Then I asked the mother: "Can Erna be of any help to her little brother yet?" The mother answered: "She can cover him up." I said admiringly: "She is already able to do this? If this is so, you do not have to worry at all when you go out, since you know that your big daughter can take care of her little brother so well. She will soon be able to attend to more difficult things. Fritz will soon recognize his sister, she will tell him many pretty things, and he will learn from her how to speak."

If at first she was not enthusiastic to see her mother go out, she did not, however, vomit again. Formerly she had been afraid to remain alone, and resorted naturally to methods of defense. But at present it was much easier for her to stand solitude and the absence of her mother, since there was now for her a prospect of activity and success.

In order to help the child realize that she, too, can become brave and self-contented, I asked the mother to come with the child for a short visit to me. When they came, there were about fifteen persons in my house, and despite this unexpected situation the child was and remained friendly. I took her on my lap, and she played with a box that was standing on the table. When I noticed that she wanted to keep the box, I said to her: "I am sorry that I cannot give you the box, but so many children come to visit me, and they all want to play with the box. Next time you come to see me, you will be able to play with it again." Without saying a word and without feeling depressed, she returned the box to me. Soon she discovered several things that interested her and which she gathered together, with great delight, on a stool. Bearing in mind the shortness of the visit, the mother came up to the child with her coat. I said then: "I believe that Erna will put the things back in their place." And sure enough she placed the things approximately where they belonged. She then gladly allowed her mother to dress her and remained friendly.

The child offered no resistance to my proposals obviously because I spoke to her in the same tone as one uses with grown-up persons. My words addressed to her contained no "must" only "may" and "can." That the flash-light would burn again only tomorrow did not imply a prohibition meant for the child in contradistinction to adults, but a recommendation to be respected by children and adults alike. It therefore involved nothing that could hurt the semsibilities of the child or degrade her. In this way, she was cheerful, without showing the least inclination to combativeness. Although I enjoined upon her certain things which she might have found unpleasant on other occasions, she bore me no grudge. When I came to her house again after an absence of some time, she said to me in a welcoming tone: "Perhaps you will remain here the whole day!"

What vexes and irritates most children is their supposed inability to do things. As soon as they notice that they are recognized and appreciated accordingly, they become reconciled to the fact that they are small. The best way to remove educational difficulties in the case of small children is to recognize their accomplishments unreservedly, even if this means nothing more than their readiness to cover up a younger brother.

SEXUAL CASES IN CHILD GUIDANCE CLINICS

By Sophie Lazarfeld

AMONG the numerous cases of children and youths brought to our guidance clinics, a large place is occupied by those apparently manifesting sexual difficulties. Nowhere do we find so much confusion and misunderstanding as in this domain. We shall therefore show by means of a few examples that these cases present only a part of the general difficulties besetting children and youths, and that accordingly they can be removed only by changing the general attitude of each particular personality.

The complaints generally refer to onanism, to strongly accentuated and intensely active sexual curiosity; in isolated cases, also to sexual delinquency. In all cases it is possible to show that these disturbances never occurred in isolation, but always in connection with other bad habits.

Adults, however, pay much more attention to symptoms of this nature than to other difficulties, presumably because they themselves are intensely interested in them and perhaps also because the memory of their own unfortunate sexual experiences prevents them from approaching sexual education with the necessary candor and impartiality. Their partiality is the source of two serious educational errors. In the first place, all questions of sex are carefully avoided by them and surrounded with mystery, since they still represent for them a dark sovereign power. This certainly more than anything else is apt to stimulate the curiosity of the child. In the second place, they put off the child with untrue answers whenever he asks anything of his own accord. A double harm is thus done to the child. He is made to suspect that there must be something unbeautiful and obscene about everything connected with sex. For he does not fail to notice that adults have a weighty interest in hushing up these matters, and he knows from his own experience that people try to hide only those things of which they are ashamed. The child is in this way given the worst possible guidance and preparation for a task in life which can be solved not by itself alone but only as a part of the whole human personality. No less harmful to the child is his loss of confidence in his fellow beings brought about by the discovery that he has been told lies. Proud of his knowledge, he is eager to display his recently acquired wisdom before his comrades. But to his consternation he meets with nothing but ridicule: his comrades are better informed than he. Not so easily does he get over the painful defeat and with a sure instinct he lays the blame for it at the doors of his mother or the person who prepared this situation for him through false statements. In this way he comes to connect sexual matters with the injustice done to him by adults. His mind is now bent upon revenge. And it does not take him long to discover that in this domain parents and educators can be hit hard.

We must also keep in mind that parents and educators who fail in sexual preparation will hardly be successful in other domains. Every child that has been sexually misguided can be expected to have a series of other bad habits which go back to other educational errors. In this expectation one never errs.[1]

SEXUAL PRECOCITY

A girl, eight years old, was sent to one of our guidance clinics. The complaint was that she indulged in sexual attacks upon other children and also upon adults. The horror of the family was naturally very great. The child herself was all permeated with this impression and her state of mind was one of the deepest fright. Fortunately she had resorted not to flight but to defiance, and all educators know that this is a less serious symptom. To be sure, the situation at first looked quite alarming. There were aggressions on all lines, against human beings and objects alike. Tables and chairs were upset, a bowl with candy was emptied of all its contents at one single grasp, the sweets were put in the mouth all at once with the greatest avidity, etc. And this was accompanied by incessant noise and cry-

1 See particularly Wexberg, "Das Sexuelle Problem" in "Technik der Erziehung," Verlag S. Hirzel, Leipzig. Lazarfeld, "Sexuelle Erziehung" in "Richtige Lebensführung," Verlag Montz Perles, Vienna.

ing. Her facial expression, however, was not at all in harmony with the spirit of destructiveness appropriate to such a wild activity. She was rather shy, did not face me directly, looked at me to a certain extent from a corner, as if she wanted to ask: Is this enough or shall I let myself go a little further? I behaved in a thoroughly passive manner and waited to see what would be the outcome. This unusual attitude on the part of an adult who does not scold, who does not resort to his greater force in order to suppress noise, who does not threaten with punishment, had the obvious effect of confirming the child in her opinion that she had not done enough and now she rushed up to me. She climbed upon me, trying to throw me down. She resorted now to "sexual attacks," making efforts to open my dress in order to look inside, etc. The repertoire was complete; by my waiting I induced her to display all her tricks before me at once. In this way I achieved two things. In the first place she became tired and was rather inclined to transact with me upon a new basis, and in the second place, I was able to gain an insight into her real intentions. As a matter of fact she now spontaneously proposed to play. It is true, in this play we were supposed to tear apart arms and legs. This marked our first hour. There was almost no conversation between us.

The subsequent course of my treatment of the child confirmed to the widest extent the opinion which every guidance worker trained in Individual Psychology will form on the basis of the description of this first meeting. The child stood in open protest against her whole environment. She felt that she had nobody upon whom she could rely, and unfortunately she really had no one who treated her in a fairly decent manner. In addition to this, her family constellation was the worst imaginable. She was the oldest of three children, not pretty, unfriendly; the younger sister was very beautiful and by nature a typical "soul-captor," as she was called by the family, which always contrasted her with the elder girl. The affairs of the family were quite ruined by disease and private troubles.

Since the medical examination to which she was at first submitted showed no somatic disturbances, we immediately applied a pedagogical treatment on the basis of Individual Psychology.

As a result of our efforts, the child pretty soon quietened down, although relapses took place regularly—a thing that was to be expected. The picture of the first session was reproduced with photographic faithfulness. The child tried to put her hands under her own dress or under that of other people, she tried to press herself to other people. These manifestations, however, never appeared in isolation. They were always connected with an attempt at aggression, she threw down fragile things, tore and injured toys which had been especially prepared for the occasion, etc. It was evident that the child wanted to be unpleasant and transferred this to a domain which was most important in the eyes of adults, as she had found out exactly. The comparison between her and her younger sister which always turned out unfavorably to her, led her to lose all hope that she could ever make herself pleasant. She endeavoured now to assert herself in the opposite direction. Naturally she over-compensated herself in her dreams, wishes, and plans. She was always a princess, the richest person in the world, explicitly emphasizing that every one would then have to obey her and that other people should have nothing. She also wanted to buy all the candy in the world in order that nothing might be left for anyone else. On this occasion I tried to make intelligible to her the relation between work and success. But she declared bluntly that she did not want to work, that everything was to be given to her. She showed no discontent with her feminine role; she said, on the contrary, that she would never like to be a boy, for men have to work, and this is the worst thing in the world.

In correspondence with this attitude was her work at school. But an improvement soon became noticeable here also. Through the help of an intelligent teacher it became possible to secure for her, in the domain of the school, that support by environment which is of such a decisive importance. Gradually the family also began to function better, and the child was able to make surprisingly rapid progress in every respect. The best visible sign of the improvement brought about by our treatment was shown by the following fact. The child laid down a little work which she had done already several times (after she had at first refused to do this or anything in general), politely asking for another work which would require more effort. At first I thought that she wanted to show off, but the perseverance with which she performed her task showed me that I was unjust to her and that I was confronted with the first success. Henceforth, things moved rapidly ahead, her character changed fundamentally, the wildness and excitability subsided, her whole behavior, even her external appearance became more amiable, the "sexual attacks" disappeared entirely. The treatment went on for a year and took place twice a week. Apart from school vacation it was also interrupted for several weeks by the sickness of the child, which fortunately did not bring about any relapse. The following year the child occasionally came to see me at the clinic and in the third year she lived in complete peace with her home and school, and the "sexual precocity," on account of which she was brought to the guidance clinic, did not show itself again. Not a single word was said to the child during the whole treatment about her "moral transgressions."

SEXUAL CASES IN CHILD GUIDANCE CLINICS

ONANISM

Guidance workers are again and again shocked by the all too frequent cases which report that children "still persist in practicing onanism, despite the fact that their arms and legs are tied during the night." Onanism is certainly only one among numerous bad habits which has to be treated like all other similar habits, namely, by not paying any special attention to this fact as such and carefully examining it in connection with the general causes underlying it. But to tell this to parents means for us quite often to run the risk of losing their confidence, and consequently, of not seeing the child again. Nevertheless the parents must be told this, since only in this way can we help the child. It is hardly possible to conceive how stupid people are in this respect. A governess came once to our guidance clinic asking for enlightenment. She wanted to know why the child of whom she was taking care (a boy of seven years) every night had both his arms stretched out and tied to a board; the parents refused to give her any information. She had just attended a lecture on sexual education and in this way she has begun to suspect the connection. Our conversation brought out the fact that she had never before heard about onanism. It was possible in this case to exercise some influence upon the parents through the governess. Of course we did not accomplish very much, since we were unable to reach the parents directly. We have, however, mentioned this case in order to show how great the ignorance is in places where a thorough understanding is so necessary.

In a second case we were also able to treat the child and parents through the intervention of a governess. But here it was a question of a person trained in Individual Psychology. It was also fortunate that she had a chance to remain for a long time alone with the child, who was also seven years old. The boy improved considerably during this time, but with the return of the parents he relapsed.

SEXUAL DELINQUENCY

A girl of fifteen years was brought by her mother to our guidance clinic, because she was a sexual delinquent. According to the story of the mother, it was not safe to leave her alone for a moment, and despite the fact that she was constantly watched, things did not improve. We immediately noticed that the mother and child lived in open conflict. The girl was very stubborn, answered none of our questions; it is true she had no chance either, since her mother constantly interfered and either answered herself, or instructed the girl as soon as a question was put, to give a "nice answer." Our inquiry into the case established that so far no sexual process had taken place at all and that it was the mother's imagination that was mainly responsible for all the to-do. Because the girl strongly resorted to masturbation the mother was afraid that she would not stop at this if she were to come nearer to boys and therefore she thought it best to keep the girl in a state of segregation.

Upon further inquiry we learned that the mother herself had eloped at the age of sixteen, had as a result given birth to this child, and had been compelled to marry the father of the girl —a thing she had been deeply regretting ever since; she had been divorced for a long time and now blames the man for the difficult situation.

She repeatedly told the story to the girl, always adding: "You are entirely like your father." The girl had reached a stage where she regarded herself as completely lost and she said frankly: "My mother has always been saying that I was no good, I shall now show her that she is right." To treat the mother was out of the question, she was absolutely insusceptible. The greatly feared delinquency would very likely have taken place, had good luck not led the girl to a different environment. She developed there excellently and her behavior has been irreproachable despite the absence of any supervision. We first learned about the case two years ago. The girl has been coming to us ever since from time to time. She is energetic, friendly, and shows no sign whatsoever of delinquency.

I should like to mention here another case on account of its special significance, although it was not treated by me, but in the teacher's guidance clinic of Dr. Alfred Adler, where I took down the report. Like a magnifying glass this case shows clearly how the origin and growth of sexual delinquency is determined by personal and social inferiority.

It was a question here of a girl of thirteen years whose father is an unskilled laborer and formerly drank a great deal. The mother suffers from tuberculosis of the lungs and from nervousness. The child was born out of wedlock when the mother was seventeen years old; the girl is followed by four other children, the youngest of whom is not quite two years old. The girl knows all about her illegitimate birth, and is in general completely informed about sex matters. She thus tells us that her mother, after she has spent the night with the father, is in a very bad mood the following morning, and that she vents her ill-humor on her. The child acts in the same way towards her younger sisters. Otherwise she feigns innocence and ignorance and she behaves very complacently and submissively towards her teacher. She stands alone in the class. The bigger girls try to get into contact with her, but she wants to associate with the teaching staff only. She is very sensitive, easily hurt. Her success at school is on the whole not bad. Her German compositions are long, highly disconnected, phantastic, and faulty.

One day several children of the class reported

that she was pursuing them with impossible and disgusting stories. She told them that she was having sexual relations with a boy of thirteen from the neighborhood, as well as with her brother who is nine years old; that she was going out in the evening with men in order to make money; that she had already been in a hotel; that she was enjoying this greatly; that this was harmless as long as one was not yet unwell; that her father scolded her for this, but that her mother looked upon this mildly and even sent her out to "make money."

When the girl was taken to task, she at first tried to deny, but after some time admitted everything except the story about the prostitution. About the latter story, she said, she was only bragging. The mother of the child appeared or pretended to be highly astonished, and claimed that she knew nothing about it. In our conversation with the girl we tried to explain to her how much harm she was doing to herself and how important it was for her own good to reform. The other children now had special reasons for avoiding her; she feels that she is being outlawed and retaliates by depreciating them blindly and maliciously.

After some time the mother was invited to the school in order to report about the girl. Not much of an improvement was noticeable. The mother now admitted everything. She had begun to realize the situation only recently. She found out that the girl was really going out with men in the evening, that several times she came home late; that she had seduced the younger children of the family and had had sexual relations with them; that formerly she used to steal and lie; that the father was not good to her and that he openly preferred the other children; that she welcomed the prospect of going to an institution of correction, with which eventuality the mother had threatened her.

The experienced guidance worker knows that he is confronted here with a feeling of depressed personality, which does not shrink from anything in order to assert itself. He regards the sexual delinquency of the case as one of numerous means to a definite end, a means which is, to be sure, especially valued because the child quickly notices and takes into account the importance attached by adults to such things.

The cases mentioned here show of what decisive importance it is for the healthy development of the child to regard sexuality not as a state within a state, but as a part,—to be sure a very essential one, but still only a part,—inseparably connected with all the other mental and bodily occurrences taking place in the totality of human personality.

RIVALRY AMONG CHILDREN OF THE SAME FAMILY

(Two cases from the Guidance Clinic of a Teachers' Association. Adviser—Dr. Alfred Adler).

By Regine Seidler

THE educator trained in Individual Psychology knows that failures and difficulties can be expected whenever the child is in danger of being overwhelmed by a feeling of inferiority. It often happens that such a child displays irreproachable behavior and does good work in an environment where he feels sure of himself, whereas he drives people to despair by his recalcitrancy in an environment where he is not sure of himself; for instance, in the sphere of his family. Such an attitude was manifested by a girl of eight, who was a paradox both to her parents and to the teachers at the school. At the request of her parents she was brought by her teacher to one of the guidance clinics.

Frieda, who is the eldest of three sisters—the others are four and one years old respectively—is quarrelsome and mischievous in the highest degree. She must always have her own way, and she tyrannizes over the whole house. If the father is served more soup than Frieda, there is a scandal in the house. Her clothes are never good enough for her. If her wishes are not fulfilled promptly, she becomes furious, she cries, rages, turns everything upside down, and even threatens to awaken her younger sister. The parents are at their wits' end.

In contradistinction to the story of the parents, the report of the teacher sounds entirely different; it has nothing but good words for Frieda. She is very nice at school, orderly, obedient and industrious. She loves her teacher and is ready to fulfill every wish of hers. The parents also confirm the fact that she goes to school with great enthusiasm and that she wants to dress as early as five o'clock in order to be in time for school. She is very intelligent, a good pupil, and is greatly loved by her comrades on account of her amiable character.

How shall we explain this contrast?

The adviser: Since when has Frieda been behaving in such a recalcitrant manner?

The mother: It started when she was four years old. At that time I gave birth to my second girl, and I had no time to bother much with her.

Adviser: Had you not previously somewhat pampered Frieda?

Mother: It was not so bad; the grandmother stays in our house and she used to allow her many things.

Adviser: Does not Frieda say sometimes that you love the younger sisters more than her?

Father: Naturally! She always believes that she is being wronged. But she gets everything she needs. She is also very rude towards her younger sisters.

Adviser: What do you do if Frieda is so disobedient?

Father: I punish her. I cannot help punishing her. It won't do to let a child of eight quarrel with her parents. When I come home in the evening from business, I want to have peace. I am nervous, have headaches and must rest. But then Frieda starts her antics. Day in and day out the same excitement. She naturally gets a thrashing.

Adviser: But by beating her you have so far accomplished nothing. I am convinced that you like Frieda, as much as the other children. But here everything depends on Frieda's opinion. The girl erroneously believes that you favor her sisters unduly. She acts exactly in the same way as an adult would act in a similar situation. She fights for her place, she tries to assert herself by the means with which she is acquainted. It does not pay to engage in a fight with a child, for the child always remains the victor. The child knows very well that you cannot kill her. You certainly have the best intentions in the world in punishing the child, but the child sees in the punishment only a confirmation of her supposed degradation.

Mother: We have also tried to be mild with her, but it all proved useless.

Adviser: This is because the child believes that she must assert herself, that she must fight. This error must be removed from the child. If you don't mind, I shall try to explain this to Frieda. You know how good she is at school. Fights are here superfluous, for here she feels quite sure of herself. She acts in a way which perfectly corresponds with her conception of her situation. Whenever she feels that she is menaced she fights, whenever she feels certain she is calm and does good work. I would advise you to go away for a few days with Frieda, but with Frieda alone, if this is possible for you. Then explain to her during a walk that you like her as much as her sisters, that the sisters, however, need more attention since they are small; tell her also that you are very proud of your big daughter who is such a proficient pupil. I believe that Frieda will give up her combativeness if you talk to her in such a spirit.

The mother expressed her willingness to follow the advice.

The adviser speaks in a similar vein to Frieda. He points out to her that she, as the oldest, could help her mother especially in taking care of her younger sisters. Frieda gladly promises to come back in a month and report about the help she is expected to give.

As a result of the light thrown by the adviser upon the situation, Frieda's behavior no longer appears paradoxical, it is rather natural and logical. How important it is for the further development of the child to elucidate the case properly can be seen from the following consideration. Were Frieda to be deprived, through a change of teachers, of the favorable ground which she occupies at school, she would lose the last remainder of self-assertion which the school at present offers her. She would inevitably be pushed to a goal on the useless side of life. Quarrelsomeness and insolence would become her instruments of fight at school also. Finally, discouraged by the disappointments following in the wake of a useless struggle, she would throw up the game. Escape from learning, complete failure, would be one of the sad results which Frieda would reap from the error.

We give here a second case in order to show how the feeling of inferiority of a boy expresses itself in all its manifestations—dreams, love affairs, recollections of childhood.

Fritz is a boy of twelve and a pupil at public school. He sees a rival in his older brother who is eighteen years old. The father of the children is in a sanatorium for consumptives, the mother is a dress-maker and supports the family. The older boy is a cap-maker by trade; he is very delicate, sickly, and is unable to stick to a position for any length of time. The mother makes allowance for his poor health. This makes Fritz feel that he is being discriminated against, and he has, therefore, been resorting since early childhood, to various kinds of mischief as a means of compensation. The punishments which his mother metes out to him do not call forth in him any hatred against her, but exasperation against his privileged brother, who according to Fritz, rejoices over his troubles, instigates the mother against him, and is in general malicious, conceited, and domineering.

At school Fritz had no difficulties previous to his fourth year, when a change of teachers took place. The stricter atmosphere which now prevails at school discourages him completely, and his hidden feeling of uncertainty and inferiority distinctly comes to light now. Fritz becomes a bad pupil. The mother is "alarmed" by the fact that he cries at night and makes himself wet. He does not trust himself to enter a dark room. But in spite of this he displays great self-assurance in his public appearance and a good deal of arrogance towards his teachers, a thing which he evidently learned from his attitude towards his brother.

Quite significant are his recollections of childhood. The father goes with both sons on an outing to a high mountain and allows each boy to hold one of his legs.

His feeling of inferiority makes him escape both in reality and in thought from every work requiring effort. In this way, he thinks that he would deposit his money in banks and live like a nobleman on the interest if he were rich. The same tendency shows itself also in his "collecting" and his greed for money. He tries to make money without performing actual work, for instance, by arranging lotteries. The tendency to have problems solved in the most convenient way possible —an obvious result of discouragement—can be seen from the following dream: Fritz together with his friends is on a boat which is anchored to the shore. Suddenly the rope gets loosened, and the boat goes cheerfully into the sea. This shows how Fritz wishes others and eventually chance, to solve difficult problems for him.

Fritz displays a similar tendency in the manner in which he tries to meet his present predicament. He is invited by a fellow-pupil to have a sex experience. But he saves himself by confessing everything to his teacher. In this way he has provided himself with an alibi which may prove useful in case the story comes out.

His feeling of weakness is accompanied by a certain noble gesture which is to raise him above his comrades. Being opposed to their predilection for football, he indulges in the exclusive sport of playing tourist, parading with his knapsack loaded in camp-like fashion, and utilizing information obtained from guides who, however, had to exclude him on account of his quarrelsomeness.

It is explained to Fritz at the guidance clinic that the special favors which his mother apparently bestows upon his brother are due to the latter's frailty. He realizes that his love affairs betray lack of courage on his part, and he is encouraged to perform positive work. Above all, his present conflict is solved in a discreet manner, which thus prevents the danger of an aberration into homo-sexualism.

A CASE OF DEAF-MUTISM

By Elly Rothwein *and* Dr. Arthur Holub

GRETA, a girl of four years, was brought to one of our guidance clinics by her mother, who complained that the child was unable to speak.

The medical examination yielded no organic symptoms.

From our conversation with the mother, we learned that the father of the child, a laborer, had gone to France to work immediately after the birth of the child because he could not find a job in Vienna. The mother, therefore, devoted all her time to Greta. The child was well developed bodily and understood everything spoken by the people around her, but she expressed her wishes by signs only. The mother reacted to the signs and learned to interpret the child's movements and glances, so that a kind of sign language grew up between them.

We explained to the mother that her readiness to react to the signs merely saved the child the trouble of learning to speak. Naturally, a general lack of independence went hand in hand with the speech disturbance. This case clearly shows the symbiosis of the pampered child with the mother, as well as the a-social isolation, of which deaf-mutism is a symptom. The mother was given directions for the removal of the disturbance, and she was specially advised to ignore the signs of the child and to make her express her wishes in words. The child herself was taken to a child community conducted on the basis of Individual Psychology, and in this way she was gradually freed from the symbiosis with her mother.

After a year she had a considerable vocabulary at her disposal, and became otherwise more social.

THE ONLY CHILD

By Dr. Alexandra Adler

THE situation of the only child is in general unfavorable. It is true, there are no other children in the family that can be preferred to him or that can push him into the background. On the other hand, he is threatened with the danger of being thwarted in his development by the excessive love and anxiety of the parents. Above all, he becomes accustomed to his role as autocrat. And since he, in contradistinction to other children, lacks early practice in sociability, he naturally has difficulties in later life. We know from experience that parents are so carried away by excessive love for their children that they rob them of every opportunity for activity. They nip in the bud every independent manifestation of will. Such children are deprived of a chance of performing the most natural activities. They are never encouraged to dress, to wash, or to eat by themselves, for they are dressed, washed, and fed until an advanced school age. Even in their play, which is the most private domain of childhood, they are never left alone. Even here parents must interfere, continually instructing, criticizing, telling the children that they know it better. It is obvious that no child can learn in this way to appreciate his own power, let alone acquire confidence in this power—that is to say, confidence in himself. Badly hampered in his aspiration for greatness and power, he tries now to attain his end by other and indirect methods. The child upon whom food is constantly forced demands now to be fed, and in this way he makes his parents his servants. The sense of power acquired in this way offers him a compensation for the unpleasantness caused by the forced feeding. The habit of shirking difficulties, however, leads the child to the a-social side of life.

The means which the child chooses for strengthening his self-consciousness, for asserting himself in his environment, and finally, for turning the attention of his environment to himself, are various. They can be passive means, such as amiableness, timidity, anxiety, even escape to sickness, or they can be active, such as talkativeness, defiance, insolence, combativeness. With all these and many other means the child fights against his environment and tries to dominate it as well as his own feeling of inferiority. This can be seen from the following cases:

KITTY

Kitty is five and a half years old. She is characterized by her mother as insolent, obstreperous, talkative, and garrulous. Kitty must know everything that is going on in the house. She butts into every conversation, and through her gossip and habit of telling things which are not meant for the ears of strangers, she is often the cause of unpleasant situations.

If any information is refused to her, she cries until she gets what she wants. Kitty is too wise for her age. She tries to utilize every opportunity to be in the center of society. She believes that she can attain this best by imitating the gestures and expressions of grown-up people. She also criticizes the actions of adults. Once, when her mother refused to give her information, she said: "I do not see why I am not allowed to know this." And on another occasion, when the mother slapped her hand, she said: "You are a nice mother! If you were my child, I would not beat you."

In the guidance clinic Kitty makes the best impression. She is vivacious, rich in imagination, and communicative. She gives a detailed answer to all questions. She obviously enjoys the fact that people concern themselves with her.

According to the mother, Kitty has a great desire for doing any kind of work. In her play, she likes to cook and to wash, although these things are not quite pleasant, since they make her dirty. The mother believes that she is rendering a special service to the child by saving her work, and she tries her best to keep the child away from the ordinary concerns of family life. When Kitty wants to be informed about what is going on in the house, she is told: "You are still a small child, it is not necessary for you to know this; when you grow up, you will be able to speak about everything, like mother and grandmother." Kitty does not acquiesce so easily and gives insolent answers.

At kindergarten she behaves excellently. The teacher has not enough praise for her.

The following conversation in the guidance clinic is characteristic:

Adviser: Where do you prefer to be, at home or in the kindergarten?

Child: In the kindergarten. There I have learned to read letters, to draw, and I also play.

Adviser: This is fine, one can see at once that you are a sensible girl. What do you do when you are at home?

Kitty: My mother does not allow me to cook, therefore I am angry with her.

Adviser: Why does not your mother allow you to do these things?

Kitty: Because I get dirty.

Adviser: You can afford to wait with your cooking, you will be able to learn this in a school for domestic science. You certainly know that your mother has to wash your clothes when you make them dirty and she has plenty to do as it is.

Kitty: My mother has bought me a pencil.

Adviser: You see how your mother is concerned about you. Does it ever happen that you do not speak nicely to your mother?

Kitty: Yes.

Adviser: What do you say to her?

(Kitty gives no answer).

Try to remember, you are such a clever girl.

Adviser: That is good. If bad words occur to you, it is best to forget them and not to say them, otherwise you only vex your mother. (Kitty meanwhile takes off her coat and puts it together in an orderly way.) This is very nice. Are you also so orderly at home?

Kitty: No, at home my grandmother does it for me.

Adviser: Try to do it by yourself. Otherwise, your folks will begin to believe that you cannot do it yet. Are you not already a big girl? If you only try, you will be able to manage it. Try to help your mother in some way or other.

Kitty: I shall cook and wash.

Adviser: Can you do anything else?

Kitty: I can make chains.

Adviser: Then make a chain for your mother, it will give her joy.

When Kitty came to our guidance clinic the

next time, she told me that her mother liked the chain very much.

We advised the mother to make the most of her daughter's zeal for work, and also to appreciate her achievements so that it would not be necessary for her to resort to insolence and gossip in order to bring people's attention to herself. We also recommended to her not to speak in the presence of the girl about things which she is not supposed to know. We told her that she must not quarrel with the child, because this only strengthened the child's defiance; that the girl has to be treated like an equal member of the family, in order that she may feel that she is regarded by her parents as grown-up; that above all, the child must not get the idea that the parents feel vexed over her insolence.

After a short time, we succeeded in changing the mother's attitude. The parents were thus able to check the girl's exaggerated striving for superiority by making her co-operate in house work; and Kitty, who now had a chance to satisfy her self-consciousness in a natural way, gave up her old and improper methods.

PAUL

Paul is eight years old. He lost his father when he was two. Since then he has been living with his mother and grandmother. The mother tells us that she would have preferred a girl. In any case, in the first years of his life he behaved like a girl. He was, at that time, quiet and obedient; he even embroidered a nice cover and played a great deal with a girl from the neighborhood. It is only in later years that he became rude, wild and irascible. Spanking did not help matters. In the morning he would not want to get up, and if we did not help him to dress he would be late for school. His breakfast he would only gulp down, he would not eat his lunch and supper decently, either—he always wanted coffee and doughnuts. When he played with other children, he always wanted to be the most important person, otherwise there was trouble; on such occasions he was quite rough. Once in an outburst of anger he threw an open pocket-knife at one of his playmates, but fortunately nothing happened. On another occasion it occurred to him to throw a lasso over his grandmother and he nearly strangled the old woman.

At school he was quite a good pupil. He might have done better in several things. Here and there he lacked the necessary patience, perseverance, and carefulness. He was enthusiastic about arithmetic and, above all, about athletics; he did not enjoy reading very much. "Reading is only for girls." He had difficulty in adjusting himself to the school community. He was one of the smallest pupils in the class, and he was not very strong. But in spite of this many of his schoolmates were afraid of him. He made up for his lack of strength by his pluck. It was he who generally started a fight and who always refused to stop; and he had no scruples in giving an additional blow to an already defeated adversary.

The following conversation shows the attitude of the boy:

Adviser: What kind of games do you prefer to play when you are at home?

Child: I cannot play well in the house, I prefer to play on the street.

Adviser: With whom do you play on the street?

Child: I have my friends there.

Adviser: Do they also go to school with you?

Child: Oh no. These are all older boys; the youngest of them is already learning a trade, he is so big.

(He indicates the size of an adult.)

Adviser: And they also play with you?

Child: Of course. When I need them, I go to Gauss Square and whistle; they come then and do everything I arrange.

Adviser: Do you meet the boys only when you whistle?

Child: Yes, otherwise they are not there, they all live on Praterstern. (Praterstern is half an hour distant from Gauss Square. Paul knows only one boy of eighteen years who plays the violin with him and now and then goes over his school work.)

Adviser: I believe that these boys are not the proper friends for you, simply because they are so far and you surely cannot always whistle to them. Try perhaps to get a friend among your school-mates; you would also be able to do your school work together.

Here is another conversation.

Adviser: What is new? What happened at school?

Child: Kurt has broken his head.

Adviser: How did it happen?

Child: He attacked Fritz, who is now my friend.

Adviser: But one does not get a broken head that way?

Child: I grabbed him by his leg and pulled him, and like a fool he fell down.

Adviser: It is very nice of you to come to your friend's rescue. But look here, you are so frank and honest in other things; you must also be so in fighting. You certainly know that boxers and prize fighters observe strict rules and see to it that no harm is done to anyone. When one makes a single false and dishonest move, one cannot continue fighting and one has lost the game. This you must always keep in mind in your fighting. No dishonest moves in order that your partner may not be injured.

The mother is advised not to beat the boy and to give him as much freedom as possible. What he can do by himself, he should do by himself. She shall not help him to dress, even if he were to run the risk of being late at school now and then. It would be well to regard him as the man in the family and to act accordingly.

Paul comes gladly to the guidance clinic. He is still somewhat combative, though by no means as rough as he used to be. If he happens to have bad luck and causes someone pain, he regrets it afterwards. He is also becoming more adjusted to his school community, and there is hope that in time he will give up his a-social attitude entirely.

TRUDE

Trude, an only child of ten, is brought to one of our guidance clinics by her father. The story told by the father is as follows: The mother has just died, after a sickness of a year. The child had been taken to an orphan asylum but ran away from the place secretly and had come back to her father. The administration of the asylum had, in any case, decided not to keep the child any longer, since she was unable to adjust herself to the communal life of the institution. For some time now she had been in the habit of telling lies, dressing with great care and taking great delight in telephoning to acquaintances and relatives telling them phantastic stories, such as, that she has lots of money, that she is about to go to America with some man, that she has travelled in an aëroplane, etc.

At the guidance clinic the child, by her manners, gestures, and expressions, gives the impression of a grown-up self-conscious lady. We learn that she began to go to school rather late on account of sickness and that she is therefore only in the third grade. However, she is happy among the little girls in comparison with whom she is grown-up and mature. To be sure, she has no friends. She decidedly refuses to remain in the orphan asylum and wants to go back to her father. Of the death of her mother, she speaks in an indifferent manner, displaying no signs of grief; according to the father, she wept only at the funeral.

It turns out that the mother was very nervous, quarrelled a great deal with her and was not very lavish with tenderness. To all appearances the girl must have been pampered in her early childhood, since she was always helped to dress and used to show off on the street. She was more attached to her father, since he was more inclined to satisfy her need of affection; it was he who helped her with her school work. But he was home only in the evening, and in this way the child was left to herself all day—a fact which accounts quite well for her precocity.

It is now a year since this change took place in the character of the girl, that is to say ever since the time her mother fell ill and her father had to devote all his time to the patient. The following fact is characteristic of the attitude of the girl towards her mother. The child was once sent to a restaurant to fetch food for her sick mother, but she came back after two hours without the food.

Explanation: The child was confronted with a new situation; the only human being to whom she was attached had devoted himself exclusively to the person who had disappointed her. The growth of the feeling of uncertainty gave rise to lying, which clearly shows Trude's discontent with reality as well as her isolation; the habit of boasting and telephoning bears witness to an excessively enhanced aspiration for self-assertion.

Unfortunately, the future of the child seems to be quite precarious, since her external circumstances are sad. The father is out of work, a foreigner, and spends his time at the tavern. For the present we have succeeded in having the child spend her afternoons at a center conducted on the principles of Individual Psychology.

THE HATED CHILD

By Martha Holub *and* Dr. Arthur Zanker

ONE summer, Fritz G. a boy of thirteen was brought to the hospital by his physician for the purpose of diagnosis and treatment. The written recommendation of the physician read as follows: "This patient suffers, chiefly at night, from such violent attacks of pain in his ears, teeth and head, that his screams are heard all over the house. The pain is not amenable to the influence of the customary medicines and it must be either of a purely nervous nature or may be caused by trigeminus neuralgia or by a tumor in the head. Since this state often lasts for several hours and since the boy gives the impression of serious suffering, we urgently ask you to give him a place in the hospital."

The anamnesis made by the hospital also established that this pain, which had been going on for two months, was of a very violent nature, that it took place mostly at night, starting in the teeth and gradually extending over the ears and forehead so that the boy had the feeling as if some one were squeezing his head. The attacks were said to have the same intensity for ten or fifteen minutes; then they would subside for a while, only to begin anew. The patient screamed so hard that he waked up the neighbors, and his mother, who is a janitress, was compelled to take the boy to the hospital at the urgent request of her employers.

The family anamnesis brings out the following facts: The father is confined to an institution suffering from an incurable nervous disease. The mother suffers from a catarrh on the extremities of both lungs and she is very nervous. The boy himself was treated for lung trouble in the same hospital when he was four years old, and spent a year and a half in a sanatorium for lung diseases.

The internal and neurological examination of the boy, which was carried out in a thorough manner, turned out completely negative. The suspicion of an ear disease was eliminated through repeated examinations by specialists. The findings of the opthalmoscope, which was applied twice, also showed a normal eye background, and in this way the possibility of a brain tumor was excluded. Nor did the examination of the teeth offer any somatic basis for the strong attacks of pain. The Wasserman reaction was negative, and thus the organic findings, except for a slight sensitiveness to pain on the part of the pressure points of the trigeminus, had to be regarded as completely negative.

It is only after these findings that the doctors set out to determine whether the case was to be regarded as a nervous or psychogenic disease. The next thing that suggested itself was to proceed in the customary clinical manner and to gain certain supporting points for this view from the external appearance of the boy—from his style of behavior, which seemed to be of the so-called reaction type. Perhaps this high-strung, very intelligent boy might better be classed with the asthenic type, the so-called sensation type of Kretschmer, or put in the category of the "vegetatively stigmatized constitution" in the sense of Bergmann, since we have here a symptom of a clear bradycardy (pulse of 66), although further vegetative-somatic symptoms of over-stimulation were lacking. Other and more distinct symptoms suggested that the case belonged to the B-type (basedowoid) according to Jaensch. The boy had vivacious, vivid, protruding, and shining eyes, a thyroid gland slightly above normal, and an extremely unstable nervous disposition—well-known criteria of the biological type which presents the strongest psychogenic responsiveness, and in which, as Jaensch himself says, strong psychological stimuli lead to the psychogenesis of bodily symptoms, and in extreme cases to genuine hysterical reactions. If one wanted to place the nervous attacks of this boy in an established classification, one could place them, on the basis of a superficial consideration, among the "neuropathies of the sense system," after the fashion of the child neurologist Cimbal, who in general places all such attacks of pain, especially fake headaches, navel colic, growing pains, and the localized radiating pain, in this class. For all these neuropathies Cimbal simply suggests a therapy of a medicamental and physical nature. This method was therefore tried in the hospital just as it was applied previously in the private treatment. But, as we have already said, it proved futile. A further step which laid more stress on the psychic origin of these attacks, namely the attempt made at the hospital to establish an acute "psychic" trauma, had to be recognized as insufficient. It turned out that there was a case of trauma, and in fact a sexual trauma, for before the appearance of the attacks there occurred some homo-sexual trouble (which even had a legal aftermath), and since this experience coincided approximately with the attacks, a connection suggested itself. How little light, however, this "sexual trauma" was able to throw upon the neurosis of the boy, will be seen from the further psychological investigations of the case, which was transferred to one of our guidance clinics.

Our inquiries into the history of the family brought out the following facts: The boy is an illegitimate child. His father, who is at present in an insane asylum and whom the boy still remembers well, (he saw him last five years before) is a Jew, and belongs to the educated classes (he is said to have studied medicine). The very illegitimacy of the child already contributes to a large extent, according to our experience, to the creation of a-social tendencies. As in numerous cases of this kind, the child lacked the normal experience of having a mother, since from his first days he grew up in boarding houses. According to what the mother says, these boarding houses were frequently changed—he nowhere fared well—a circumstance which hardly helped him to gain a sense of security.

After we had established these facts, we tried to find out, in accordance with the customary practice of Individual Psychology, the child's *style-of-life*. We know that children can be divided into certain definite groups according to the ways in which they utilize their experiences. Now our first problem was to what group does this boy belong? The abnormal childhood of the boy as described above clearly suggested that the boy belonged to the class of so-called "hated children." For not only was he, as an illegitimate child, denied the normal experience of having a mother, but as a boarding-house child he also had to suffer sad experiences which developed in him the erroneous belief that everyone in this world was hostile to him. In this way he arrived at a very pessimistic outlook which left a mark upon his whole character.

As luck would have it, there took place one day an extraordinary event in the life of Fritz. He found himself one fine morning in Denmark, where he was sent with a group of other children. There he spent a whole year as an only child in the house of a well-to-do family, which treated him as their own child, and lavished upon him attention and love. Fritz does not tire of telling what a princely life he led there and of his experiences with ski-parties and mountain excursions. He had the best time of his life there, and his only desire now is to go back to Denmark. We must keep in mind the contrast between these two events in the life of the boy. On the one hand, the boarding-house period with its scoldings and beatings giving rise to a consciousness of a life stunted in love and hence to a constant hunger for affection; on the other hand, the Copenhagen period, a paradise in which this hunger found complete satisfaction, but from which, alas, he had to be banished too soon.

We have to imagine now the state in which

the boy found himself after his return to his mother's home. He finds that conditions at home are miserable, more miserable than they were before he left. His mother, meanwhile, has become a housekeeper, and on top of that has married another man. The present husband, moreover, is a cab driver, a decent but uneducated man (the mother herself stresses this fact). She once said: "My first husband was a very educated man, but my present husband is uneducated." The boy is unable to become intimate with him (so far he has not kissed him even once, according to the mother); rather, he has an attitude of superiority towards him. Matters are complicated here by religious differences. For the first husband and the father of the boy was a Jew, while the second husband and the mother are Christians. The situation becomes especially difficult for Fritz through the fact that a brother comes into the world. The younger child is now four years old, seems to be greatly pampered and presents himself as the well-known type of the "obedient and kind" child. The mother utilizes every occasion for emphasizing the difference between the two and for singling out the younger one as her favorite. As was to be expected, this state of affairs gives rise to the characteristic secret conflict between brothers, to a rivalry which Fritz betrays to us in his comments upon the situation. Fritz naturally believes that the younger brother is being preferred to him in every respect, and also often complains about the fact that he gets little to eat, etc. Fritz is carried away by this rivalry to such an extent that he even once threatened to kill his younger brother. The experience of the preference given to a second brother only gave new nourishment to a fundamental tendency which had its roots in the early childhood of the boy, since even then he always felt that he was discriminated against, and that he got too little. The new experience naturally was digested in accordance with his style of life.

His attitude of superiority towards his family, his sensitiveness, and his habit of fault-finding assumed more and more unpleasant forms. We can quite well imagine that he felt out of place at home and that he tried with all his might to get out of the house. Nothing meets with his approval at home; he begins to nag and tyrannize over his mother. Ever since he returned from

Copenhagen, as his mother tells us, he has become more and more fastidious—especially as far as food is concerned. For his breakfast he must always have cocoa, and when his mother brings the cocoa to his bed he complains that it is too hot and wants her to cool it off. He then continues sleeping, and the mother has to bring him the cool cocoa and wake him up again. He makes a great deal of noise at home, but when someone begins to talk aloud, he immediately shouts that he wants to have rest. He is becoming more and more domineering, is disobedient, comes home unpunctually, does not tolerate any criticism, but rather blames his mother, telling her upon the slightest provocation that she has a grudge against him. He sometimes even frightens his mother with his threats of suicide, and once he actually made an attempt to jump from the third story.

It may appear strange at first glance that the boy's behavior at school is exemplary. He learns things with particular ease, his teachers are greatly satisfied with him and regard him as highly gifted. He is conspicuous for his talent for drawing, and he seems to possess the necessary qualities for the calling of his choice—he would like to become an expert mechanic. This example again shows us clearly how a neurotic arranges everything in his life in a way which best suits his purposes. To be the best pupil, and to acquire rich stores of knowledge are things which correspond excellently with his secret aspirations to rise eventually from his present miserable circumstances to a better place in social life—like the social life he experienced in Denmark. But success at school was not enough for him, he also wanted to be superior at home. One of the chief methods resorted to by neurotics in order to attain that goal of superiority and to shirk the duties of social life, is backwardness in learning. But this, as we see, is out of the question for our boy. He cannot use this method.

It has become impossible for Fritz to stand reality—that is to say, the life at home, which has been irritating him more and more since his return from Denmark. Given the life-style of the child, it is not surprising to see him resort to illness as a means of escape to the useless side of life. He has chosen illness for this purpose because he was already familiar with the advantages of being sick, through his sojourn in the sanatorium for lung diseases during his childhood. We are therefore not surprised to hear that his violent attacks of pain begin about this time. The above-mentioned "sexual trauma" fitted in quite well with this mood. To believe him he was nearly seduced, and this charge against the environment seemed to be a perfectly intelligible justification for his grudges against the world and for his flight from it. He told us once in connection with this question that in his opinion the world was bad. The homo-sexual attack thus lends countenance to his escape from reality.

The violent attacks of pain described above, began about this time. Suddenly the boy started to complain of headaches, shouting: "I am suffocating, I have no air!" He screamed so loud that many tenants in the house threatened his mother to deprive her of her position as janitress; they are reported even to have complained to the board of health. It is to be noted that besides exasperating the tenants, he also in this way keeps his own family at bay. We admire here, as in similar cases, the ingenuity, the high grade of intelligence, with which the neurotic plays his game. By means of these attacks Fritz really completely succeeds in realizing his secret aspirations for superiority, for keeping the whole family under his thumb. The mother must be at his disposal day and night. These attacks bear specially hard on the father, who comes home late at night, tired and greatly in need of rest, since he has to get up at four in the morning. Everything in the house must bend to the boy's whims. The bed must constantly be changed around despite the smallness of the apartment, the door must now be left open, now be closed. During the day he runs home and wraps himself up in shawls, because he has great pain; at night the pain subsides if he can go out and for this purpose he must have the key of the outside door.

What therapeutic measures could be applied to this neurosis built up with so much ingenuity? Above all, how was the boy to be extricated from the meshes of an erroneous life-plan? We must point out that we are able to succeed here only by calling into play several educational factors. A great deal of the credit is due to the advisers themselves, but specially to the assistance of a student. As a tutor of the boy, the student was in the habit of taking Fritz for walks several times a week. In this way he was able to carry on the spirit of the work of the guidance clinic; he also had a chance to supply us with very important material owing to his intimate contact with the home and personal life of the child. In the second place, great service was rendered here by the public character of the guidance. In this way we were able to stimulate social feelings in the child and also to secure the active co-operation of the outsiders that were present at the guidance meetings; among these a special role was played by an American family that became greatly interested in the boy. In the third place, the family itself and particularly the mother proved helpful.

It is true, the mother at first even put obstacles in our way. Despite all our efforts we were for a long time unable to inspire her with faith in the successful outcome of our work. She always concluded despondently: "There must be a nervous trouble in the boy." She often repeated, in the presence of the boy that he must have inherited this trouble from his father, that "the boy has the same whims as his father." Our first impression was that this very intelligent woman, who even in the first conversation complained that she had seen better times, whose whole being plainly showed that life had not treated her any too gently, was not fit to cope with the child. And the boy himself seemed to have detected that the nerves of his mother were too weak (as she herself also admitted). In her attitude towards the child there was a certain contradiction which she obviously was unable to overcome. On the one hand, she attended to him with great tenderness; on the other hand, she had nothing for him but words of reproach. It was only at the cost of great efforts that our guidance workers were able to enlighten this fainthearted, despondent mother about the causes of the child's neurosis and to win her over gradually to our side.

Before we started to change the boy's pessimistic outlook, we tried, in accordance with our usual procedure, to make clear the position of the boy within the family and to perform first the easier tasks; for instance, to transform the rivalry between the two brothers into a tolerable relationship. After a short time we succeeded to such an extent that the older boy was willing to take charge of the younger child and he even enjoyed his task. We were, at the same time, able to bend his rigid ego-centric attitude. The boy became interested also in the wider world around him, which formerly had given him no joy. He even became heartily attached to his tutor and he felt very happy about the connection he had established with the children of the above-mentioned American family, who invited him to their house and played with him. To be sure he was still too conscious of the fact that he occupied the center of the stage, that he was an interesting case that attracted wide attention. How beneficial this general interest must have proved to him can be seen from the fact that he came to the guidance clinic more and more cheerfully, obviously craving for this attention.

Indications of his pessimistic outlook are furnished by his childhood recollections: He was tied to the leg of the table by the lady with whom he boarded, before she went out shopping. The same attitude is displayed in a free composition which we asked the boy to write for us. He describes here an unsuccessful outing—he was pursued by bad luck and had continually to look for protection.

In order to change this pessimistic attitude, we showed him, by means of concrete illustrations, that people were well-disposed towards him, and how certain people were interested in giving him joy. He was, for instance, lavishly presented with stamps. At every session in the guidance clinic, some member of the audience always gave him stamps, and Fritz, being a stamp collector, was greatly interested. The American family became more and more concerned about him, and the tutor became more and more attached to him. The Copenhagen dream was coming true!

We were, nevertheless, well aware of the fact that this advantage would also inevitably entail a disadvantage. Fritz had somewhat changed his pessimistic outlook. He told us once in this connection that he had been mistaken, that he no longer believed that all people were bad. But this sudden change of attitude, this joy over the generosity of his friends, involved the danger that he might forget that one must give joy to others to the same extent as one takes and receives it. At a certain moment when we believed the boy to be sufficiently mature for such considerations we utilized the culminating point of his new optimistic state of mind to convince him of the truth: He who takes must also learn to give. Above all we tried to bring home to him the fact that he must be especially considerate to his mother, that he must make it his aim to give her pleasure. And approximately at the same time —not earlier—we endeavored to make the boy realize and understand his previous errors, especially the connection existing between his boarding period and his present behavior.

He understood this explanation quite well, as often happens with children. It was clear to him now that he had acted on the belief that having been given too little, he had therefore constantly to grab more. He realized that he was mistaken in thinking that his mother preferred the younger brother to him. It was only then that we found it advisable to indicate to him the real meaning of his attacks of pain. We showed him that there was a purpose to his attacks, that by disturbing the peace of the house at night he meant to compensate himself for everything of which he had been deprived, that he had chosen an irrational road to his goal, instead of realizing that every one must put up with reality even if things do not go as they did in the fairy-land of Denmark. We constantly gave new form to these explanations which seemed to fall upon fertile ground. At the same time we tried to encourage him as much as possible; the drawings which he brought to us always met with sympathy and approval.

As a result of this transformation and this change in the state of mind, this "inner conversion" (to use an expression of Schulze) which forms the necessary condition for the curing of every neurosis—the boy began to lose his neurotic symptoms. After the later guidance sessions his headaches became more and more rare (of course, we never spoke about them in the presence of the boy), and soon disappeared entirely. The gentle toothache in the lower jaw, from which he could not separate himself entirely, was to us quite a familiar strategic device for covering a retreat, a last place of refuge.

Of a more serious, though transitory significance, was another occurrence which took place in the meantime and which led to a renewal of the attacks. This occurrence deserves special mention, because it again demonstrated that the basis of the attacks of pain was nothing but psychological. Otherwise they would not have reappeared so promptly in consequence of an event of a psychic nature. The occurrence thus had for us the value of an experiment. The American family to which the child was so attached departed one day without taking leave of him. This was all the more surprising as the boy had made arrangements with the children of the family for an outing. The disappointment of the boy must have been very keen. The attacks suddenly appeared at this time with their old intensity, and the mother came again to us in quite a despondent and hopeless mood. We had to spend a good deal of effort in order to patch up the new rift and to enable the boy to regain his equilibrium. As bad luck had it, the court proceedings in reference to the homo-sexual case in which Fritz had to appear as a witness, took place about the same time and naturally gave rise to additional excitement. We utilized the accident with the American family, we even welcomed it as opportune, in order to strengthen the boy's sense of reality. We tried to show the boy that we were not greatly astonished at this event, that such things happen in life, that one has to reconcile oneself to such facts. We also expressed our conviction that the sudden departure of the Americans must have been due to some urgent circumstances—to disease or to some sad accident—that in all probability they had not had time to say good-bye to him, and that they would certainly write to him.

Since that time the attacks have again calmed down, and have not reappeared for the last two months. But we nevertheless continue to follow with great interest everything that Fritz or his mother has to tell us. We want to be modest enough to assert that we initiated a change in the state of the boy's mind and that we removed in this way painful symptoms. But we are also aware of the fact that we must continue to assist the boy in the future and as long as possible, because we want to make sure that his present adherence to the useful side of life will remain permanently.

ESCAPE TO DISEASE

By Dr. Friederike Friedmann

ANNA, who is thirteen years old and is physically well-developed, is, according to the report in the guidance clinic, remarkable neither for good nor for bad work. One day she gets spasms in her heart, because, as she herself told us, a classmate of hers had badly hurt herself in falling down, and the sight of it had greatly upset her. She is immediately taken home where she is attended to with great care by her family. She stays away from school for two days. A few days later she gets another similar attack, but this time she is kept in school and put to rest. She then wants to go home by herself in order not to frighten her parents, but she has nonetheless to be accompanied home, because she collapses after a few steps. One thing was rather surprising in this connection: she stepped rather firmly into the machine that was to take her home. She is again absent from school, this time for only one day. A week later, she gets a third attack, which is accompanied by such violent crying that every one is puzzled. The school physician of the neighborhood who happens to be in the school building, is sent for. His verdict is: "Escape to sickness."

The antecedents of the case: Anna is the second of four children. The two younger ones are babies. A few weeks ago the family saw the birth of another girl, whom Anna by no means welcomed with joy. She had to stay away from school for some time, because she was needed at home, but since she was not a particularly bright pupil anyway, she missed, in this way, a great deal and was afraid that she would not be able now to get ahead. This discouragement over her school work was strengthened by the consciousness that she was entirely superfluous at home. The older sister, who had till then been her friend and play-mate, became indispensable in the business that had always been managed by her mother, and accordingly she had no time for Anna. Moreover, Anna herself, who had been pampered in the past as the younger sister, was not only not asked to help take care of the baby, but she was frankly kept away from the child, since she was not considered reliable enough. Anna now felt that she was neglected, she felt also that she was incapable of offering any real help, since she had been accustomed during so many years to the role of the youngest, pampered daughter who leaves everything to the care of her mother and elder sister. She also lacked the necessary courage in order to make up for what she missed. She started with spasms of the heart, because their frequent recurrence secured for her the care and attention of the family. That the attack took place precisely before the arithmetic lesson, this touch-stone of all the fainthearted, shows clearly that the thing was arranged by the child.

The treatment proceeded in accordance with the indirect method so often used by Alfred Adler. When Anna was resting on a couch apparently exhausted from pain, apparently also indifferent to external impressions and influences, the difficulties falling to the lot of a girl through the birth of a younger sister were discussed with all the people who came to see her. It was pointed out in this conversation that disease increases such difficulties and that much courage is required in order to assert oneself under such circumstances. Twice Anna listened to this quite passively, but the third time she raised her head and said calmly and with self-possession: "This is true but not entirely so." There was another factor here, as she said—namely, her teacher had not allowed her to associate with a new friend.

Conditions at home soon became more favorable for Anna as a result of our conversations with her older sister. By means of tutorial assistance she was enabled to fill the gaps in her knowledge; various class offices with which she was charged seemed to give her a higher standing at school.

About a year later she complained of pain in her right arm. She had fallen down and as a result she injured the joint of her right arm. When she was examined, her first words were: "I have not done it to myself in order to avoid work." And in order to show her good faith she kept on working, despite the swelling, even in the drawing lesson, which formerly she had longed to miss. She had a new drawing teacher and was afraid lest she fare badly. The general situation, made easier for her through the weakness of the hand, the admiration paid her for her persistence in working and drawing with a swollen hand, helped her to regain her mental equilibrium.

Anna has not yet changed her life-style completely. But she knows what it is all about, and she satisfies herself only with telling about her great bodily suffering whenever she is confronted with a difficult situation, not shrinking, however, from work. The admiration reaped by her for her proficiency and resoluteness supplies her with the courage necessary to assert herself beside the elder sister who is so greatly appreciated, as well as beside the baby who is so much liked.

TWO CASES

By Dr. Lydia Sicher *and* Martha Holub

EVEN A SINGLE CONVERSATION MAY BE SUFFICIENT

L.M., a girl of six years, is the youngest child and has two brothers considerably older than she. The mother complains that she can never go out in the evening, since the girl refuses to sleep as long as the mother does not go to bed. Whenever she wishes to obtain anything from her mother she always whines, and she is very insolent towards her brothers. Upon further inquiry we learned that the girl generally makes great demands upon her mother, that she has to be helped to dress and to wash, that she has to be taken home from school.

At the guidance clinic we explain to the mother and child the life-style of a pampered person, which corresponds to the behavior of this child. We point out that the baby-like attitude of the child towards her mother has as its purpose to remain in a state of dependence in order to be able to dominate the mother. The provocative attitude which the child assumes towards her brothers shows, in the opinion of the advisers, that the girl, pampered as she is, doubly resents the superiority of her brothers. Her apparent insolence is only a mask for lack of courage.

At the next session the mother reports that the evening following the first meeting the child spontaneously expressed her willingness to go to bed alone. "I never imagined that she would change," said the mother. During the whole week she was so nice towards her brothers that she wondered what had happened to her. She also tried hard to be independent, and of all her previous symptoms she retained only her whining habit.

In our conversation with the child we tell her that we understand quite well that it is not so easy for her to give up her baby-like behavior at once. We urge her to judge for herself whether there is not a contradiction between her childlike whining and her general behavior, which corresponds to that of an adult. We appreciate her efficiency and stimulate her to further activity.

THE "TRAUMA"

Mrs. F. is a frequent visitor to our guidance clinic. So far, however, she has not had enough confidence to bring along her little daughter, who is four years old. Her questions betray the fact that she takes great care of her child. They refer mostly to food value, that is to say, to the composition and quantity of various food articles. This suggests to us that the child must have eating difficulties. Our suspicion indeed proves to be true.

From our conversation with the lady we learn that she has already mapped out for her baby daughter the career of a singer. She had, so she tells us, several physicians examine her larynx, to which rays are being applied now in order to strengthen it. Naturally the mother is greatly afraid that by speaking aloud, let alone by shouting, the child might injure her precious organ. We try to explain to the mother that she is mistaken in her attitude, that by her methods she jeopardizes the development of the child, and may eventually cause her great disappointments.

The next time the mother reports to us in despair that her daughter was so frightened by a friend who had put on a mask that since that time she has been refusing to remain alone even for a moment. Having at our disposal the material that the mother had supplied us, it was not difficult for us to show the mother that it was not the "trauma" that was responsible for the present condition, but the erroneous life-style of herself and her daughter's, and that the experience served only as a pass-word for the release of a symptom. The nature of the "difficult situation" in which the child was involved was not quite clear to us. One thing was, however, obvious, that this situation was created by the pedantry of the mother who imposed upon the child requirements which she could hardly fulfill. Our assumption that the child was neurotized by the neurotic mother was soon confirmed by the mother's own confession. She told us, namely, that she herself was afraid of remaining alone, that she always had to invite a cousin to stay with her overnight when her husband was away, since she was afraid that a man might come down from the roof through the window. In this way we had an opportunity to tell her something about the purpose of fear, and as a result of our discussing means for correcting fears in children, we were able to educate an adult.

A CASE OF SPEECH DISTURBANCE

By Dr. Alexander Müller *and* Dr. Theodor Vértes

HANSI R., a girl of nine years, is the younger of two sisters; she was introduced to us on October 16, 1928.

The occasion for the introduction: rapid decline in school work; hired out as an errand girl in a shop, but concealed the fact from her mother and was spanked on that account.

Environment: The father died of paralysis five years ago, constant excitement at home in the last year of his life. The mother lives on a pension, characterizes herself as very nervous. She is painstakingly orderly, an extremely talkative nagger, yet kind. The sister is thirteen years old, industrious, quiet, orderly, congenial, reads a great deal. There is also in the house an old aunt of eighty who causes difficulties for Hansi by her antiquated views and by pampering the child. The family lives in simple but regulated circumstances; the cultural level is average.

Organ inferiorities: malformation of the palate, hare-lip, protruding lower jaw, farsightedness, squinting (high glasses), crooked teeth, left-handedness. Speech disturbances: through a split in the palate she is partly hindered in forming sounds; she sometimes stutters so that it is hardly possible to understand her. Child diseases: measles, bladder trouble.

The anamnesis brought out further troubles which have been manifesting themselves gradually, especially since the last few months. She turns out to be extremely ambitious and vain, and also disorderly. She is quarrelsome with her sister; she provokes the mother by eating difficulties, by fumbling around, by slovenliness, by constantly wanting to be attended to, and, as a last resort, by stealing. The mother reacts with refusals, prohibitions, thrashings, and endless moral sermons. At school Hansi tries to make herself conspicuous by her restless disturbing behavior, and by her refusal to learn. As a result she is constantly punished and exhorted. The more unsuccessful she is, the more mischievous is she both at home and at school. Meanwhile she completes a course in speech treatment without any success whatsoever. This naturally makes her more conscious of the fact that she is handicapped.

The finishing stroke was offered by some sad experiences. Since she is not only unable to defend herself well on account of her speech troubles, but she cannot even pronounce a single word when she is greatly excited, she is made the scape-goat for all sorts of bad tricks. Besides, there is no one at school to take her part, since she has made herself highly unpopular. Her outbursts of rage result only in a general hostility.

Despite the fact that Hansi's position is weakened by pampering, caused in turn by her organ inferiorities, and despite her supposed insufficiency, she has the over-ambitious aim of outflanking her sister at any cost. In this way she is driven to devious paths and gradually forced to become an envious, grudging person, since she has no confidence in her capacity for competing in the normal walks of life. She gives up the race, resorting to methods by which she keeps her whole environment constantly busy.

The purpose of our guidance was to enlighten the girl about her erroneous attitude—the attitude that her only aim in life was to outdo her sister—and to change it accordingly, as well as to enable her to replace the behavior corresponding to this mistaken attitude by regular and socially useful achievements. This purpose was gradually accomplished within four months through conversations conducted with the mother and daughter every two or three weeks and through corresponding instructions and advice. We also entered into contact with her school and her general environment.

In accordance with our recommendation the *teacher* grants Hansi a period of grace during which her attempts at disturbing are ignored (and thus rendered ineffective), while her positive achievements are emphasized; after a short time she is even charged with the office of keeping order in the classroom. In this way she realizes more and more how advantageous it is to act sensibly, and how useless it is to hunt constantly for attention.

The *aunt* also yields gradually, does not pamper Hansi so much and does not always take her part in opposition to the sister. Hansi is thus compelled to bear herself the consequences of the difficulties provoked by her—a thing which is not much to her liking, since she is no longer protected, and especially since her sister avoids all skirmishes in accordance with our instructions and tries to treat her with understanding and sympathy.

The *mother* gradually overcomes her own "nervousness"; she pays no attention to the girl whenever she becomes nasty, abandoning—with one exception, which caused a relapse—all kinds of punishments. She induces the girl to do housework by constantly emphasizing that she is a great help. In this way she is stimulated to be orderly and assisted to give up her hostile attitude towards the family and work.

Hansi herself is baffled by this attitude towards her conduct. It is a surprise to her to see that the adviser takes no notice of her antics and that he only refers to her good qualities (anamnesis: she is good in sports, loves to draw, is very able and original in handwork, quick in housework), and stimulates her to further activities. At first she had declined our advice to find friends for herself. But after two months she reported, beaming with joy, that she had the whole class as friends. This, of course, she owes, in the first place, to her teacher, who induced the girls not to beat or ridicule their colleague.

The first manifestations of this success are now utilized both at school and at home. She is told that she owes these good results to her independent efforts and to the fact that she now plays and co-operates everywhere joyfully, without trying to occupy a central position, and that with continuous practice she will manage to be as beloved and as good a pupil as all the other children. The proof was furnished by Hansi herself in the middle of February. Her school record of the term read: In speech and reading, good; in all other subjects, very good. And the mother added: Hansi has really become very nice and proficient; but we all have become quieter also.

It is the full confidence with which every one treated the girl that is responsible for the rapid success.

THE EDUCATIONAL WORK OF THE PRIVATE TEACHER

By Paul Brodsky

WE know that those children who are in need of private instruction, who are regarded as lazy, stupid, and ungifted, are in open conflict with their parents and teachers. Parents and teachers seldom succeed in gaining access to the true self of such children. The educators of such children are often guided in their judgments only by external failures; it does not occur to them that the causes of these failures do not lie in the child's "bad will" or in his "wicked intentions," or in his "lack of aptitude," that these causes are rather results of a life-style which is characterized by the child's search for help, relief, and support.

In January, 1926, I undertook to give private instruction in commercial subjects to Fr. He was seventeen years old and a pupil in the first class of a commercial high-school. His external appearance struck one at first glance with its unhealthy stoutness, which made the boy look rather helpless. His forehead was in folds, his speech indolent, his face sleepy, without any expression, and dull, his movements slow, as if they were made against his will. It is also important to mention that his joints were unusually soft and flabby, with a strong inclination towards losing his balance. All this was the result of a disease of the thyroid gland (myxodema), which was constantly under treatment and which, moreover, represented a serious organic inferiority, whose effects of necessity showed themselves in the mental life of my pupil.

Fr. is the only son of well-to-do parents. The father, a lawyer of repute, is somewhat nervous and greatly concerned about the recognition of his personality. He is very much attached to his son, pampers him (for instance, he shaves Fr. with his own hands), takes him gladly into the society of adults. But all this pampering in the end reduces itself to the tendency of constantly treating Fr. as a small child, of not allowing him to grow up.

Fr. resists this tenderness. He said to me

once: "I cannot stand the tenderness shown to me by my father. It seems to me that he is not sincere. I feel as if he were constantly observing me."

This shows clearly that Fr. sees his father's tenderness in the proper light, that he experiences it as an expression of paternal authority, which again makes him conscious of his immaturity. His desire to be "grown-up" can be seen from the fact that he does not know the names of his schoolmates after he has stayed with them for two years. He kept away from these youngsters as an "adult" and in this way saved himself from immersion in the crowd. According to the report of his father, he is quite lively in his intercourse with adults and enjoys a good deal of popularity.

The consciousness of the fact that he is being observed is the expression of a "bad conscience," since he knows well that he does not perform the tasks imposed upon him; what is painful here is the feeling of the debtor that cannot pay.

I explained the father's surveillance to Fr. in the following way: "The father has engaged a private tutor; he naturally wants to know something about the work done by him. Since he cannot be present at the lessons himself, and since you supply him with no information, he has to observe your work, in order to be able to judge about my work." Besides, I showed him that he has shaped his whole behavior in such a way as to be the most observed person in the house.

How little Fr. was inclined to recognize the authority of his father is shown by the fact that he never asked him for any advice or information. The father naturally felt very badly about this. Through this distance Fr. wants to protect himself against defeats, although, on the other hand, he tries to imitate his father's aptitudes in order to be his equal. His father, for instance, has proved successful as a writer. Fr. accordingly also has his mind bent on writing, although in his attempts he naturally does not go beyond the most primitive rudiments. That he tries to combat the paternal authority which weighs so heavily upon him by depreciative attempts, is obvious. Thus he gladly tells you that his father is an unreliable person, that he speaks at table about his digestive troubles, etc.

The mother is a strong woman, resembling Fr.

in her external appearance. There is between her and Fr. a kind of alliance directed against the father; she does her share in pampering the boy, although her influence seems to be smaller than that of the father. In any case she is quite occupied with the management of the house. She is not quite well and because of this is hindered in her movements.

We can summarize the situation as follows: It is a question here of a highly discouraged boy, who, like all children, suffers from a disposition to inferiority, intensified in this case by a strong organ inferiority which has a disturbing effect upon the total functioning of the organism.

When I came to their house, the father was about to reconcile himself with the fact that Fr. was unintelligent. He was quite surprised when I told him that I did not share his opinion. It seemed to me necessary to tell him this, in order to prevent him from letting the boy fail. The father informed me that at the beginning Fr. was doing well at school, but that at present, before the end of the term, he needed assistance.

Presumably, the father wanted Fr. to learn "something" as quickly as possible, in order to procure for him, thanks to his connections, the possibility of practicing something like a profession. The study of business seemed to be the most proper means to this end. But Fr. was opposed to this, first, because it was the father's wish, second, because he was in general in no hurry about a profession. As far as he was concerned, he did not mind spending all his life in school; after all it was easier to retain one's ground at school than it was in life or in a profession, about which enough had been said to frighten him. Since the commercial school was not a difficult affair and since the director of the school was a good friend of the father's, Fr.'s state of health was taken into account and everything went well at first. But with the approach of the end of the term Fr. began to feel less certain. Up till now he had succeeded in making the parents think that everything was all right. In order to deceive himself and others in regard to the real situation, he gave no direct answer to the questions about his standing at school, resorting instead to long-winded explanations or shifting the conversation by putting questions about some other subject. If these questions were heeded, then the painful theme is disposed of, otherwise he could point out that the interest shown by him was not appreciated and that, consequently, he could not be made responsible for eventual failures. This is certainly a nice way to avoid responsibility for future failures.

During such situations, Fr.'s face is entirely expressionless, almost dull, the eyes half closed, the hands folded over the stomach, the arms indolently propped up, the whole body sluggish. He clearly tries to close himself up to everything coming from the outside as if he were not there at all. This attitude is an answer to the sermons so frequently preached to him by his parents, sermons always having for their refrain: "How often have I told you this!" Through this attitude, however, he succeeds in immunizing himself to ideas so that he need not follow them.

He does not worry over the views of his parents, since he interprets their silence as a sign of satisfaction, although at the same time he knows quite well that this is not the case.

But this gives rise to a danger. If the parents are satisfied, this means that he has reached the level expected by them, and now he runs the risk of being unmasked in view of his term record. His work, therefore, declines, so that tutorial assistance becomes necessary, in order to show that he could not keep pace with the increased requirements of the curriculum. If the bad record arrives, the blame is laid at the door of the curriculum and the tutor who was not able to prevent this; he himself is not guilty at all. In this way we can understand why things stopped going a month before the end of the term, and also why tutorial assistance was not found necessary earlier.

Since I had no reason to expect him to work outside school by himself, I had to spend our lessons in doing the work together with him. On this occasion, Fr. showed me how skillful he was in wasting time. Whenever I explained things to him he resorted, by preference, to the method of closing himself up, as described above. In this way it was not necessary for him to understand anything, and I was compelled to start my explanation anew. As soon as I discovered these tactics, I tried to elicit an interest from him by putting questions. But when Fr. noticed that I wanted him to be interested, he tried to deceive me by attempting to prove—and at great length—errors or incorrect answers. Thus he attempted to prove that America was situated to the east of Europe by declaring that one could reach America by continuously going eastward. With this method of demonstration he aimed both to waste time and also to achieve the triumph of apparently being in the right and hence to procure for himself for a moment the feeling that he was superior to me. In this case it was possible for me to induce him to give up this view by telling him that the Eastern route could be used but that the Western was the nearer one. I should like to mention in this connection another example whose importance will appear later. When Fr. noticed that I was interested in his photographic pictures—I had special reasons for this, as will be seen later—he showed me his pictures at the beginning of every lesson, accompanying them with long-winded explanations. That this was only a means for shortening the lesson became evident as soon as I proposed to postpone the exhibition of the pictures until the end of the lesson.

Exercises formed a special chapter. Only very rarely did he make any for his school, and not very often did he prepare any for me, although I insisted upon this. I explained to him that the exercises assigned to him had been planned by me so that he might easily find the necessary material in case he wanted to practice.

Since he regarded the exercises as a compulsory measure, and since he did not believe that he was able to do them by himself, he found it necessary to resort to all kinds of explanations for his failure to perform them. He availed himself here of all the customary tricks. Now he had lost the page with the note, now he poured ink over my assignments, he did not even shrink from petty frauds; for instance, changing my assignments. When I told him that I saw through all his tricks, he admitted this, but resumed his old tactics after some time in the belief that I had already forgotten about them. His tendency to make others responsible is especially seen in the following example. In order to stimulate in him an independent study of civics, I proposed to him, knowing his ambition for authorship, that he write an editorial about the rights and duties of citizens. He was quite enthusiastic about it, especially since I left the thing to his discretion and set no date. About a week later I happened to come to the lesson late. Fr. was furious; he was afraid that I might make up for the time missed by staying longer. I assured him that he had no reason to worry, and asked incidentally for the article. "I wrote it," he said, "but I haven't got it any more." "What has become of it?" "I tore it to pieces and threw it into the fire because I was angry with you for not coming on time." But since he was already in a conciliatory mood, he added that he would positively write it for the next lesson. This "positive" assurance was, however, a good sign that he had not written it at all.

It was inevitable for me to strike upon these tricks, and I showed him in fact the mechanism of his attempted deceptions. It was, however, only towards the end of his second year at school that he began to give up these tactics. Soon he began to bring me only complete work. He was supposed to hand in a school exercise in arithmetic. I proposed to Fr. to use my method for this purpose in order to test its practicality. For each of the six days which he had at his disposal I gave him five examples—thirty altogether. He was to solve them immediately after his mid-day nap. Fr. accepted my proposal and on the sixth day he brought all the examples with an air of triumph. In order to show how proud he was of this achievement, he wrote all the examples with red pencil. He also wanted me to show his work to his father, which I naturally did. Almost fifty per-cent of the examples were correct, only a very small part showed mistakes in the statement of the problems, that is, lack of understanding.

This work proved to be successful, but never again did he use my method, for this was liable to lift him to a higher and responsible level, to bring him nearer to a happy termination of his school career, and hence nearer to "life." He rejected everything that could lead him ahead. Otherwise it would be proved that he, too, could and had to do things. For my praise of the stenography teacher, he had nothing but a depreciatory remark: "It is not meant sincerely." During our stenography lesson he would take down as many as fifty syllables a minute, while at school he would hardly go beyond forty. I wrote down for him precise rules telling how to proceed in separate numerical operations. He was supposed to use these rules whenever he had to solve problems for his school work. He lost the paper with these rules. I gave him a second copy, which he used for contriving "crib" notes for his school work. I checked up these crib notes: he naturally used them wrongly—a small attempt at making me responsible again.

I was anxious, in view of his future career, to protect him against a possible failure in his examinations. I therefore discussed with some of his teachers the subjects in which he would be examined. It was left to me to set a day for the examinations. But nearly always when I decided that he was ready, his examiners had difficulty in letting him pass. It was against his will that he passed his examinations. This fits in clearly with his fight against everything that was liable to bring him nearer to the solution of the problem of choosing a profession.

Before I take up this problem of a profession, I should like to give a few more examples of his father's educational methods.

Fr.'s father, who is a good pianist, also lets the boy study piano. The tendency on the part of his joints to upset balance shows itself strongest here. In spite of this he was forced by his teacher to play through his scales fluently, and his father supported this method, at least in Fr.'s early years. The father reports that he used to watch Fr.'s playing very closely, that he counted up in order to find out whether the boy was playing a scale sixty times in succession; he wonders now why the boy refuses to practice, and why he hates classical music and prefers only to play dance music.

The father gives Fr. pocket money, but he has to account for the way in which he spends it. I induced the father to let Fr. do typing for him at his office and also to pay him for his labor without asking him to account for the money, since this was personally earned by him. Fr. gladly availed himself of this opportunity, spending his money on radio and photographic outfits.

Soon after I gained Fr.'s confidence to a certain extent, he declared to me that he wanted to become a photographer and that he did not want to work in an office. He indeed spent a great deal of time on this occupation and developed a number of pictures, although none could be used at that time. This was evidently a side-show, meant to serve as a means for evading the tasks imposed upon him by his father, with a view to the future calling chosen for him. The father did not want to hear of photography, and tried his best to spoil his son's appetite for it. With Fr.'s consent, I began to work upon his father. I pointed out to him that it was not necessary for Fr. to start upon a career at the age of eighteen, that there was no difference between a business employee and a photographer. I succeeded in changing the father's attitude by telling him that Fr. might find a job in a film enterprise, if he had a good photo-technical training. I was also helped by the fact that there was in the house all the apparatus left by a deceased brother of the father who had graduated from a photographic institute. (This explains how Fr. came to the idea of photography). As an expression of his consent the father bought for Fr. an enlarging apparatus, and from that time on his pictures gradually began to improve. He developed faultless pictures, which the father always carried in his brief-case; they were pictures of persons whom Fr. regarded for some reason or other as superior to himself: parents, relatives, teachers, acquaintances, etc. This shows that photography is an excellent means for satisfying one's feeling of superiority. For it certainly depends upon the photographer whether the object in the picture is pretty or not; he is able to arrange expressions, posture, bearing and finally, through an unsuccessful picture, he can revenge himself upon his oppressors. But of me he never made a good picture. The first picture was without a head, the second did not come out at all, because he had forgotten to put in a film, the third was blurred. At the fourth picture I asked him not to try this time, since I was not properly dressed, but he took the picture just the same. This picture was the best of all he had taken of me, although it was not quite clear; he enlarged it and pasted it in an album; I cut a rather miserable figure on it. This was a kind of revenge for a double sin committed by me; in the first place, I had won over the father to the cause of photography and in this way deprived Fr. of the opportunity for blaming the father for his failure to solve the problem of a calling; in the second place, it was I who transformed his side-show into a main battle-ground.

After I had won over the father it was necessary for me to make Fr. familiar with the new conditions. I was doubly anxious to protect him against a possible failure, since it was decided to send him to a photographic institute. He was completely satisfied with this, for this gave him two more years at school. Besides, the curriculum did not seem to be difficult either, since he had already studied commercial subjects and in the first year he had to take up chiefly drawing and photography.

Now that doors and gates were wide open to him, he tried again to block up these gates. He gave up the race completely at school, began to have for the first time since I knew him attacks of the heart, which were found by the physician to be of a nervous nature, and he had to stay in bed. He thus resorted in June—shortly before the end of the term—to an "escape" from the useful side of life.

Despite this revolt, certain results of a more cheerful nature began to show themselves. He was to take an examination in drawing, for which he was prepared by a private teacher. He had always been exempt from drawing work at school. He had fifteen private lessons and as a result he passed his examinations fairly well; the father was happy. Following my advice, Fr. became a member of the society of amateur photographers, "Urania," and took an active part in its work. What was most gratifying was the fact that he managed to finish the first year at the commercial school without special difficulties.

We may now make a summary of the case. We are confronted here with a typically pampered, only child, whose claims to special privileges seem to be justified by illness. In order to maintain the central position conquered by him when he was a small child, he uses all the means characteristic of such children, from a prearranged illness to laziness, from opposition to the parents to the "exclusion" of unpleasant facts. He has placed sentinels in all directions: distance from his father, utilization of disease, the various attempts at backsliding in his work both at home and at school, in order to protect himself against defeat. To retain his superiority at night also, he wakes up in fright, and has difficulties in falling asleep when the parents are away.

In this way he is led to assume a hostile attitude towards his environment, to regard it as a battle-ground from which he escapes, since he is afraid of leaving it as a victim only. Despite self-delusions, despite safe-guarding devices which prove to be a failure, these conflicts lead him to lose more and more hope in the possibility of achieving success and of reaching a state of real superiority; he consequently resorts to the world of dreams for the realization of his frustrated wishes. He dreams that he stands in the hall and sees something big coming down from the roof. He opens the door and sees a bear. He snatches a dagger and begins to fight with the bear, throws him over the stairway and strangles him with his bare hands. When he comes home, he finds his parents waiting for him, and the father shakes hands with him, expressing his gratitude for his exploit. Another time he dreams that he is Orpheus and that he is descending to the nether world with a harp in his hand. Of a sudden he is attacked by a herd of ghostly steers.

He strikes the chords of his instrument and passes through the herd without any fear.

The distance which he puts between himself and the problem of a career, appears to us as an everlasting preparation, for the fiction of a thorough preparation enables him to postpone its solution indefinitely. If a diverting inclination (in this case photography) which at the same time requires a more or less prolonged training, proves successful, then the inclination can be made an end in itself, whose achievement can be made desirable for the pupil through encouragement (success at the examination in drawing, the experience of friendship with the tutor). If the father furthers the activity of Fr., success can be expected almost with certainty. Fr. is thus about to solve the problem of a career.

If we expect an escape from the social problem in view of this lack of courage, Fr. will not deceive us on this score either. Since he tested his weapons at home, he avoids circles where he has to take a stand. For this purpose he avails himself of the fact that he feels superior to his colleagues, that he does not feel at ease at the dancing lesson. He has no friends.

As far as the third vital problem is concerned he has not yet been confronted with it, to speak officially, although he has taken an attitude to this also. This is what I inferred from the answer which he gave me when I asked him whether he was interested in girls. "I have not thought about it yet, I still have time for this." Can there be any doubt that he will do everything he can not to have to think of it as long as possible, until it will fortunately be too late?

In working out this case my main aim was to show that the task of the private teacher is not primarily to inculcate certain subjects in his pupil. To aim at success through drilling means to accomplish very little. In most cases where private tutoring seems to be necessary, it is a question of discouraged children whose failures are not to be explained by smaller or greater difficulties in the subjects of instruction. These subjects are on the whole within the reach of a given class age. What the private teacher has to do is to enable his pupil to realize that he too could succeed, provided he stops identifying his aim with a sham superiority, stops waging war against his parents and teachers, and musters up instead the necessary courage to show that his achievements entitle him to be treated as an equal. It is the task of the teacher to foster in his pupil such an attitude towards the problems of life as well as to make him approach them, not with a view to the mistaken attitudes of the parents or teacher, but with a view to his future place in life.

THE END

CPSIA information can be obtained at www.ICGtesting.com
Printed in the USA
BVOW07s1600271214

380982BV00001B/196/P

9 781614 271482